'Many on the Left will hate this book and reject it wholesale. A more constructive approach would be one that engages with the arguments put forward by Paul Embery, a union activist and an authentic working-class Dagenham voice.'

**Jon Cruddas, MP for Dagenham and Rainham**

'For anyone who wants to see a Labour government again, read this book. It's a bitter pill to swallow but it's essential medicine for some parts of the Left if they are serious about renewing the bond with the people they were founded to represent. Some of it will make you wince. All of it will make you think.'

**Gloria De Piero, former Labour MP for Ashfield**

'Paul Embery is a gifted writer with political vision and great courage. This book tells the story of how Labour lost its way and can find it once more.'

**Maurice Glasman**

'Paul Embery has become a key witness to the death of blue-collar social democracy in Britain. He describes how, in his home borough of Barking and Dagenham, and in British politics more generally, the combination of hyper-globalisation and identity politics has turned working-class politics upside down. Even if you are familiar with the critique of identity politics you should read this book; not only is it intellectually sharp but it is the account of someone who has experienced the change as a personal and collective tragedy.'

**David Goodhart, author of *The Road to Somewhere***

'Most voters lean left on economics and conservative on culture but no one represents them. Embery delivers a tight, passionately argued plea for the Left to rediscover its roots in social solidarity. *Despised* confirms Embery's place as a leading force in the emerging left-conservative movement.'

**Eric Kaufmann, Birkbeck College, University of London**

# Despised

For the people of Barking and Dagenham
DEI GRATIA SUMUS QUOD SUMUS

# Despised

## Why the Modern Left Loathes the Working Class

Paul Embery

polity

The right of Paul Embery to be identified as Author of this Work has been asserted in accordance with the UK Copyright, Designs and Patents Act 1988.

First published in 2021 by Polity Press

Polity Press
65 Bridge Street
Cambridge CB2 1UR, UK

Polity Press
101 Station Landing
Suite 300
Medford, MA 02155, USA

ISBN-13: 978-1-5095-3998-7
ISBN-13: 978-1-5095-3999-4 (pb)

A catalogue record for this book is available from the British Library.

Library of Congress Cataloging-in-Publication Data

Names: Embery, Paul, author.
Title: Despised : why the modern left loathes the working class / Paul
    Embery.
Description: Cambridge, UK ; Medford, MA : Polity Press, 2021. | Includes
    bibliographical references and index. | Summary: "Why the modern left
    will regret sneering at community, family and the nation"-- Provided by
    publisher.
Identifiers: LCCN 2020024550 (print) | LCCN 2020024551 (ebook) | ISBN
    9781509539987 (hardback) | ISBN 9781509539994 (paperback) | ISBN
    9781509540006 (epub)
Subjects: LCSH: Labour Party (Great Britain) | Right and left (Political
    science)--Great Britain. | Working class--Political activity--Great
    Britain. | Party affiliation--Great Britain. | Great Britain--Politics
    and government--21st century.
Classification: LCC JN1129.L32 E63 2021  (print) | LCC JN1129.L32  (ebook)
    | DDC 324.24107--dc23
LC record available at https://lccn.loc.gov/2020024550
LC ebook record available at https://lccn.loc.gov/2020024551

Typeset in 11 on 13 pt Sabon by
Servis Filmsetting Ltd, Stockport, Cheshire
Printed and bound in Great Britain by CPI Group (UK) Ltd, Croydon

For further information on Polity, visit our website: politybooks.com

# Contents

# Acknowledgements

I owe a debt of gratitude to many people for their help and support in making this book a reality. My editor, George Owers, was a constant source of encouragement and sound advice. Thanks must also go to Evie Deavall and Julia Davies at Polity for their generous assistance and all-round professionalism, and to Tim Clark for his first-rate copy-editing.

The ideas and opinions in these pages have been influenced by countless individuals, but I must give a special mention to my friends and allies Maurice Glasman, Jonathan Rutherford, Adrian Pabst, Jack Hutchison, Liam Stokes and Tobias Phibbs, with whom I have spent many happy hours putting the world to rights (often together as a group over a beer or three at the marvellous Red Art café in Dalston). Needless to say, however, not all of the views expressed here will reflect their own.

I thank friends and colleagues, past and present, in the Fire Brigades Union, particularly Lucy Masoud, Grant Mayos and Joe MacVeigh, whose comradeship over many years has meant much. I also owe a great deal to the fine team at UnHerd, especially Sally Chatterton and Freddie Sayers.

I am indebted to my parents for their support and

Acknowledgements

encouragement throughout my life. They have influenced me in ways they will probably never know.

The greatest thanks must go to my wife, Tricia, and children, Nicholas and Rachel, for their unstinting patience, solidarity and love.

# Introduction

A nation held its breath as the clocks struck ten on the evening of 12 December 2019. Many of my colleagues across the labour movement had been hopeful of a positive result in the general election. Not necessarily an outright victory for the Labour Party (only the most optimistic – or delusional – foresaw that), but certainly a hung parliament leading to a minority Labour government supported perhaps by some kind of arrangement with the Scottish and Welsh nationalists. And these days, in labour movement politics, such an outcome would have been considered a victory.

Some of the more realistic anticipated defeat. A few – such as those who stood in the 'centrist' tradition of New Labour and had never reconciled themselves to the Corbynite ascendancy – positively willed it. But hardly anyone expected the annihilation that came to pass and, with it, the devastating loss of so many Labour heartland seats.

And so it was that as the exit poll flashed up on TV screens, forecasting a thumping eighty-six-seat majority for Boris Johnson's Conservatives, the hopes and dreams of a stunned British Left collapsed. For many of the Left's foot soldiers, the next few hours would be

1

spent grimly observing the prediction turn into a painful reality – the Tories eventually secured an eighty-seat majority – as the results rolled in and the sheer scale of the wipe-out become apparent. Constituencies that had been Labour for as long as anyone could remember – in some cases, for nearly a century – fell like dominoes: Blyth Valley, Great Grimsby, Bishop Auckland, Leigh, Wakefield, Bassetlaw, Sedgefield, Wrexham, North-West Durham, Bolsover, Don Valley – the roll call was chilling.

The sense of disorientation felt by many on the Left over the following days was palpable. How could this massacre have happened? Voters had suffered a decade of austerity; Boris Johnson was a clown who had to be hidden away from the public during the campaign; Jeremy Corbyn, by contrast, was playing to packed houses everywhere; Labour could lay claim to having more members than any other political party in western Europe; the Brexit saga had proved debilitating, but there was still an energy and optimism across the movement such as hadn't existed in years. So why had working-class supporters deserted *their* party in this way?

For my part, I watched these events unfold with the same deep sense of disappointment but none whatsoever of surprise. I knew this moment had been coming: I had been warning about it inside the labour movement and beyond for long enough. In fact, just four days before the election, I had tweeted:

> Thursday will be a pivotal day in the history of the British labour movement. If our Red Wall crumbles, as some of us have long predicted, it will be a time for serious & honest reflection. If we win, then I really don't understand politics as much as I thought I did.

# Introduction

The rupture between the Labour Party and the working class was an accident waiting to happen, and one which it didn't take unique powers of observation or exceptional political wisdom to foresee. It didn't begin with Jeremy Corbyn's election as leader. It had, in fact, been brewing for the greater part of three decades – during which the party had swallowed a poisonous brew of social and economic liberalism – intensifying significantly in the second half of that period. The further the party travelled along the road to the imagined sunlit uplands of cosmopolitan liberalism and global market forces, renouncing much of its history along the way, the more it alienated its working-class base. You needed only to go to the right places and speak to the right people to understand this.

But so many in the labour movement, including those among its upper echelons, didn't go to these places or speak to these people – at least not enough. Instead, they mixed in their own exclusive circles comprising only those who thought exactly as they did. Many spent their working lives in professional occupations or the public or voluntary sector, in their spare time moving in the world of trade union committees, Labour Party meetings and assorted protest movements. They were usually rooted in the cities – especially London – and had, in many cases, gone through university. On social media, they would follow or engage with only those who shared their worldview. They confused Twitter with Britain. Some were members or fellow travellers of various far-left groups (though the further they progressed in the labour movement, the more likely they were to hide the fact).

Little wonder, then, that the Left became increasingly detached from those living in working-class communities up and down the country, and ignorant of how they think, what they believe, and why they believe it.

The handful of us who warned of impending electoral calamity were often written off by others inside the movement as 'reactionaries' (or worse) who held a 'nostalgic' view of the working class. We were told that today's working class really did desire the move to a more globalised world, in which such concepts as borders and national sovereignty were of diminished importance, traditional values – such as around family and patriotism – were obsolete, and liberal progressivism enjoyed hegemony. Well, some of them did, no doubt. But, from where I was sitting, most seemed thoroughly ill at ease with such a proposition.

I would have loved to be proved wrong. I am a democratic socialist. I want the Left to succeed and be able to address the injustices of the world and improve the lives of those it ultimately exists – or at least once did – to represent: the working class. I have always done so. That's why I joined a trade union aged sixteen in 1991 (when I landed a Saturday job stacking shelves in the Dagenham branch of Asda) and then the Labour Party (of which I am still a member) in 1994; why I became an activist in the Fire Brigades Union when I began my career as a professional firefighter in 1997 (eventually serving on the union's national executive); why I joined the National Union of Journalists when someone thought my opinions worthy of a column; and why I have spent much of my adult life participating in campaigns and activities across the labour movement.

You might say that this political partisanship was inevitable. I come from a family which, like pretty much every other family in our community, voted Labour. I have a vivid memory of my dad watching the news on TV in the early morning after the 1983 general election and griping about Margaret Thatcher's victory over Michael Foot. He was a shop steward for the old Transport and General Workers' Union at his works depot, and my mum, a secretary, later worked for the GMB union. Though I had little idea at the time what this all meant – and while neither of my parents were especially political in any broader sense – I understood from quite early on that Labour and the trade unions were good and Thatcher and the Tories were bad. (I imagine that this was what inspired my twelve-year-old self to stand as the Labour candidate in the mock general election at my comprehensive school in 1987. I won by a landslide – though I'm quite certain this was a consequence of geography rather than any personal qualities!)

If we are products of our environment, then my politics are shaped immeasurably by the borough of Barking and Dagenham and its people. For it was in this most working-class of places – part of the county of Essex before it was swallowed up by the Greater London conurbation in 1965 – that I lived for the first thirty-five years of my life, most of it on the sprawling Becontree council estate, and which provides the backdrop and inspiration for many of the ideas and opinions expressed in this book. In fact, almost all of what follows in these pages owes itself to what I learned there.

In particular, the convulsions that were experienced in Barking and Dagenham in the first decade of this century – during which it found itself thrust into the centre of a national debate over globalisation and immigration – were instrumental in forming within me an utter certainty that a major schism between the political establishment and the working class was on the cards. For I watched during that period at the closest quarters as the people of the borough were ignored or written off as racist and bigoted by a political and cultural elite who knew nothing of their lives and showed little willingness to learn.

These were my friends and neighbours. I had lived and grown up alongside them. They were mostly decent, hard-working, tolerant, people – the kind upon whose loyalty and endeavours the success and prosperity of our nation has over generations depended. Yet, as the full impact of the new global market began to take hold, and as their lives and community were subjected to rapid and unprecedented economic and demographic change, their expressions of anxiety and discontent fell on deaf ears. They soon came to realise that not only was much of the liberal establishment impervious to their plight, it actively despised them.

Everything they had ever known was suddenly transforming around them. The cheerleaders for globalisation told them it was all for their own good. They said it would bring improved GDP and cultural enrichment. But the people of Barking and Dagenham felt no better for it financially, culturally or spiritually. It wasn't change per se that they opposed; it was the sheer pace and scale of it. And if I – a young left-wing activist and member of the Anti-Nazi League who had marched against the National Front – could understand this (as I came to eventually), why couldn't the politicians who had been around for much longer?

So it came as no surprise, at least not to those of us living in the borough, when the far-right British National Party (BNP) moved in and took advantage, coming from nowhere to win a dozen seats on the local council in 2006 – the party's best ever result in local government. Just a few years previous, such an event would have been unimaginable in Barking and Dagenham. When, though, the BNP proved ultimately to be no solution to their woes, tens of thousands of locals, their patience exhausted, simply moved away. For them, the place was no longer home. They left behind a borough scarred by atomisation and resentment. Where there was once an enduring harmony, there now existed discord. A solid, stable, blue-collar, working-class community had been torn apart, its people betrayed, and few with any kind of power or influence seemed in the slightest bit bothered about the fact. As I often said to friends and neighbours afterwards, 'Someone really ought to write a book about what happened here.'

Hundreds of working-class communities similar to Barking and Dagenham can speak of their own experiences of having been neglected by our political class in recent times. These places – inhabited by proud citizens who place a high value on social solidarity, belonging and rootedness, and are often imbued with what many among the political and cultural elites deem to be outdated and uncultivated views – have become the new frontier in British politics. The quiet – and, more latterly, not so quiet – rebellion that has been fomenting in these areas is what gave us Brexit. It's what gave us the evisceration of the Labour Party in 2019. It's what has created a challenge to the dominance of cosmopolitan liberalism, which its advocates were certain represented the end point of social progress.

The people in these places cried out to those in power to heed their concerns. But for years these cries went unheard. That Labour – the party towards which so many working-class voters had for decades shown so much loyalty – was complicit in this disregard of them was inexcusable and ought never to be forgotten.

Labour was certain that it knew better than those who had supported and sustained it for over a century. The party tried to tell them what was good for them and it brooked no dissent. If the working class couldn't see the virtues of global liberal progressivism, then it was wilfully ignorant.

This mindset owes itself to the fact that there has existed for some time on the Left a disturbing level of group-think, the consequence of which is that key planks of ideology are rarely challenged and the certainty of partisans in their own moral rightness is mutually reinforced. By extension, those who dare to think or argue differently – especially if they do so from within the movement – are marginalised and abused.

This, in turn, has created a culture on the Left – one which in recent years has begun to infect public life generally – in which freedom of expression is nominally defended but is, in reality, under attack as never before. Honest debate and disagreement, particularly around contentious issues, are becoming increasingly precious. In their place, a rigid and oppressive conformity is demanded. Opinions that are still common currency across large parts of our nation have been delegitimised and effectively banished from the public square.

We have a new national religion – liberal wokedom – and anyone who blasphemes against it can expect to be vilified by its high priests and followers. Those who hold positions of prominence or influence had better be especially careful, for they risk seeing their livelihoods or reputations destroyed if they dare express dissent.

These days, arguments are frequently shut down simply by one party in the dispute claiming to have been 'offended'. Giving offence – even unintentionally and regardless of the merits of what has been said or done – is itself now seen as a sin worthy of punishment. Where we once placed a high premium on reasoned and respectful debate permitting the expression of a range of diverse and competing views, we now have echo chambers, 'safe spaces' and draconian hate legislation, all of which serve the purpose of supressing unwelcome opinions and enforcing an official orthodoxy from which nobody can expect to depart without repercussions.

It is no coincidence that at the same time as acting as the driver for this suffocating new reality, the Left has increasingly immersed itself in the destructive creed of identity politics, in which minorities are divided into discrete categories according to their race or religion or sexuality, and classified as inherent victims who must be protected from an oppressive and 'privileged' majority. This entire approach has, in practice, gone far beyond the laudable objective of defending people against prejudice, and has sought instead to promote the separateness and unique characteristics of these groups as virtuous in their own right, and the groups themselves as thereby worthy of favourable political treatment. Needless to say, all of this serves only to fragment the working class and undermine what should be the primary goal of developing common bonds and building the maximum unity required to defend its interests.

The modern Left and the working class currently inhabit separate worlds and are motivated by conflicting priorities. The fact that at the 2019 general election – after nearly a decade of Tory-imposed austerity – so many working-class voters were willing to place their faith in a Tory party led by an old Etonian instead of the party that was considered to be their 'natural home' is a stark reflection of the extent of this estrangement. Whether the Tories are able to hold on to these voters will depend on whether they improve their lives and communities in a tangible and lasting way, providing them with hope, investment and opportunity. If they do, Labour's problems will only deepen, for there is no route back to power that does not pass through these places and win back the hearts and minds of those who live in them.

There is a chance, of course, that Labour has lost for ever much of its one-time core vote. That's why it would be a fatal error for the party to assume that things could not get even worse. An organisation whose members, activists and representatives have so little in common with so many working-class voters – neither speaking their language, nor sharing their interests or priorities – can hardly hope to maintain their support. In today's Labour Party, it is the liberal left and, to a lesser degree, the far-left that hold sway – two camps whose adherents are often at loggerheads with each other in the battle for supremacy, but neither of which ultimately has the capacity to reconnect the party with its old heartlands. The party is now an organisation comprised largely of urban middle-class liberals, students and social activists; it is no surprise, therefore, that it is towards this con-stituency that its policies and pronouncements are most overtly aimed.

Labour has a mountain to climb if it is to be a serious electoral force again. And if it proves unequal to the task, it will relegate itself to being a party of permanent protest. In everything it says and does over the coming years, Labour must consider as a first concern what the impact will be in its old working-class heartlands. All policy development must be geared to this end. This will mean a sharp rebalancing of its priorities – focusing less on topics that do not command mass appeal or interest, and more on the doorstep issues that voters see as rel-evant to their everyday lives.

The party needs to combine the goal of creating a fairer and more egalitarian economy with a social programme that speaks to the instincts of millions of working-class voters. It must rediscover a part of its history of which so many of its activists today are ignorant: the early Labour tradition that spoke to the patriotic and communitarian instincts of the working class and understood that we are social and parochial beings with a profound attachment to place and a desire to belong.

This will necessarily mean discussing openly issues such as globalisation, family, law and order, the nation state and national identity, immigration and welfare, and being prepared to change position. It will mean, too, reappraising the cultural revolution that has been taking place in our country since the 1960s and assessing candidly whether everything that it spawned has been to the good.

The past few years in Britain have been a lesson in what happens when an arrogant elite takes its hegemony for granted. If you don't take people with you, if you haven't won hearts and minds, if you plough on stubbornly when millions of working-class voters are imploring you to hold back or change course, then you are asking for trouble. And, in the end, trouble came.

Our politics is fracturing. Liberal progressivism is in retreat as working-class people seek to revive the politics of belonging, place and community as an antidote to galloping globalisation and rapid demographic change. The assumption that greater economic and social liberalism would pave the way to a new age of progress, prosperity and enlightenment now looks woefully mistaken. Tribal party loyalties are crumbling as sections of society long ignored by the ruling elites start to kick back. The Left bears a heavy responsibility for this polarisation, and it is why it currently stands decimated and flirting with irrelevance.

In this book, I set out why this happened and how it might be fixed.

But first, a point of explanation about my use of the

term 'working class', which is of course interpreted in all sorts of different ways by everyday people, political activists and academics alike. Some believe it is determined by personal characteristics such as accent or lifestyle, or whether a person owns his own home or takes a holiday abroad, or by qualifications or income. Many on the Left argue that it covers all those who are forced to sell their labour in return for a wage; others get sniffy about including certain sections of the middle class – or the 'petit bourgeoisie' – in this definition. Then there is the much-used National Readership Survey (NRS) social grading system, which defines class by occupation type, with the working-class falling variously into the C2, D and E categories. Some believe individuals (such as the self-employed) should be free to define themselves as working class, regardless of other factors, if that is how they see themselves.

All of the above definitions have some legitimacy, and all have their weaknesses. There will likely never be a universally accepted definition of 'working class'. You pays your money and takes your choice.

For the purposes of this book, I have avoided any standard scientific definition except where it is relevant to the point being made. Instead, I use the term 'working class' as I have understood it all my life. I use it as many of my friends and neighbours and workmates understand it. I use it in a broad sense in the way that, I suspect, the man on the Clapham omnibus or in the Red Lion understands it – to describe the stratum of society whose members often do the toughest and most grinding jobs (consisting, for example, of physical labour or work in blue-collar industries, factories, call centres, retail or frontline public services); those whose wages and social status are generally at the lower end of the scale; those who own little or no property or wealth, beyond perhaps their own home and some modest savings; those who are likely to have little authority or control in their workplace; those who live in the grittier parts of Britain, particularly our post-industrial, small-town or coastal communities and those districts of our cities that haven't yet succumbed to gentrification or been colonised by the professional classes; those who are unemployed or more likely to be in receipt of benefits; and so on.

Given the wide variety of options, I expect some will find fault with my broad definition. That is their prerogative. But if the reader genuinely cannot comprehend my perception of what it means to be working class, and the reasons why I see it that way, I probably cannot help him. I do think most people will get the point.

I should say, for the avoidance of doubt, that when I use the term 'working class' I most certainly do not mean only the 'white working class', and anyone who infers such a thing when reading these pages has completely missed my argument. On the occasions in the text that I do refer specifically to the 'white working class', it is because it is relevant to the point being made.

My 'working class' is what might legitimately be described as the 'traditional working class' (or, once upon a time, the 'industrial working class'), but that is not a euphemism for white. It would include, for example, the West Indian who came to Britain as part of the Windrush generation and worked on London's transport system; the Muslim who settled in a Lancashire mill town; my own late father-in-law who came in the 1960s from India and was employed as a sheet metal worker; and so on. Some on the Left think such people by definition cannot be considered part of our nation's traditional working class. I think that view betrays their own prejudice.

I do acknowledge, of course, that the working class as I describe it is not homogeneous in its beliefs, and not all would have traditionally seen Labour as their natural home. Some might even consider themselves instinctive Tories. But I believe strongly that, regardless of individual party political preferences, there is a common thread running through much of this working class – one that is patriotic, often socially conservative, communitarian, rooted, and which places a high value on family, place, social solidarity and cultural stability.

All of this must be set against the emergence in Britain of what some have described as a 'new working class' – younger, urban, more likely to have gone to university, highly diverse, less politically tribal, and more liberal and cosmopolitan in outlook. I think there is merit in this analysis, as such a cohort is certainly beginning to take shape. Members of this group may have limited financial means and face many of the challenges that those among the more traditional working class face, particularly, for example, in relation to precarious employment and lack of affordable housing.

Despite this, however, I am sure that several of them would – at least for the moment – reject some of the arguments made in this book. I do not as a consequence suggest that this group cannot be considered a legitimate part of the working class; indeed, such a claim would be absurd. Neither do I suggest that the labour movement should not be responsive to their aspirations and demands. On the contrary, it is the job of the movement to build the maximum possible unity across the class.

Nevertheless, I think it fair to say that as things stand this cohort still constitutes only a minority among Britain's wider working class and, moreover, is not what the broader population immediately think of when they hear the term. Maybe that will change in time. For now though, I think my use of the term 'working class' in its more traditional sense remains perfectly valid and will be widely understood.[1]

# 1

# The Gathering Storm

'Treat people like cattle, and you'll get kicked', as the man said. The people of Barking and Dagenham had been treated like cattle for years. Patronised, neglected, dismissed. Many had disengaged from the political process entirely. The political establishment was tin-eared. It didn't want to hear from people like them. It thought they were a bit, well, uncultured. All it wanted was their votes at election time.

Among locals, the feelings of abandonment, of marginalisation, of being ignored, were profound; the sense that their views and concerns would never be taken seriously by a political class that saw no legitimacy in them was palpable.

I was a fourth-generation resident of the place. It was home for thirty-five years. Those of us who had lived and grown up in communities like this, and knew them and their inhabitants intimately, saw the revolt coming a mile off. We had warned time and again that the anger and bitterness were building. That the writing was on the wall.

And then 23 June 2016 happened.

The establishment and its outriders were shaken to their core. To some of us, though, the vote to secede from the European Union came as no great surprise. In Barking and Dagenham, 62 per cent voted Leave. The cattle had kicked. It was their response to a ruling class that had long regarded them with contempt. Their way of getting their own back.

For Barking and Dagenham, read hundreds of similar working-class communities across post-industrial, small-town and coastal Britain. These places had had enough. For years, they had been treated as social and moral outcasts by the political and cultural elites. The sneering derision of these elites was summed-up in the words of *Times* columnist Matthew Parris after he paid a visit to Clacton-on-Sea in Essex in 2014: 'Clacton is going nowhere', Parris opined. 'Its voters are going nowhere . . . This is Britain on crutches. This is tracksuit-and-trainers Britain, tattoo-parlour Britain, all-our-yesterdays Britain.' As if maligning them mercilessly were not enough, he went on: 'I am not arguing we should be careless of the needs of struggling people and places such as Clacton. But I am arguing – if I am honest – we should be careless of their opinions.'[1]

Parris expressed openly what many of his chattering-class political and media chums believed privately: the people of Clacton and communities like it were trash and not worth listening to.

Some political and media commentators would have us believe that the divisions and strife that have plagued our country in recent years began on referendum day. On the contrary, they had been brewing for years. The EU referendum was merely the mechanism which enabled the populace to give full vent to their festering anger. They had waited a long time. Like magma rising quietly and unobserved inside a volcano, the pressure was building. Yet the political establishment was blind to it. Until the day the eruption occurred.

Despised

How, then, did we get here? What were the origins of our current tribulations? Why did a nation that to outsiders may have appeared harmonious and at ease with itself begin to experience such convulsions?

## *The rise of the cultural revolutionaries*

It may seem something of a stretch to some, but many of the seeds of Brexit and the wider polarisation of our nation were sown back in the 1960s. That pivotal decade saw a seismic shift – a revolution – in political, social and cultural attitudes across the Western world. The origins of the rebellion lay in the universities, where thousands of students – the bulk of whom hailed from various sections of the middle class – rose up against the old order. Their protests culminated in a sustained period of revolt throughout 1968, with Vietnam of course a great galvaniser for the dissenters. But they had much more than US imperialism in their crosshairs.

Old-fashioned concepts such as patriotism, self-discipline, conscience, religious belief, marriage and the centrality of family, manners, respect for tradition, personal morality, and a belief in free will – all of which had, over many generations, become so firmly embedded in British society, not least as a consequence of the country's deep roots in Christianity – were being rejected wholesale. And in their place came the beginnings of a new age of free love, drugs, self-gratification, individualism, divorce, contempt for tradition, and disdain for the concept of personal responsibility for one's own actions.

The old universal moral code, which broadly united people irrespective of their class or political beliefs, and the breaching of which was certain to induce shame,

18

was slowly breaking apart. The cultural revolutionaries were on the march.

The spirit of the age came to be summed up in the lyrics of the song 'Imagine', penned by 1960s icon John Lennon. 'Imagine there's no heaven . . . no countries . . . no religion too . . . Imagine all the people living for today.'

All of this was done in the name of 'liberation', of course. It always is. The revolutionaries considered their causes entirely worthy and themselves inherently better people than those against whom they waged a culture war. And in some respects they were right. But, like many battles for liberation, the invoice didn't arrive until many years after the event, and only then did people see the price to be paid. What was presented as 'peace, love and harmony', turned out in so many ways to be the opposite.

It is important to say that one does not have to be a social reactionary, nor hark back to some mythical 'golden age', nor believe that we are living today through some dystopian nightmare, to believe that the new morality hasn't proved in every respect to have been for the better. And, of course, not all modern-day social problems can be attributed to the legacy of the 1960s. Indeed, it would be absurd to postulate such a thing. An ever more predatory free-market capitalism, with its culture of long hours, low wages, overwork and stress – and the impact of these things on family life – has unquestionably taken its toll on society and contributed in no small part to our ills.

Neither is it credible to deny that sections of the working class have themselves embraced some of the more tawdry aspects of cultural liberalism and a shallow consumerism which have undermined social bonds and deepened the moral decline. We should be honest about the vices as well as the virtues of the working classes, and there is no room for romanticism in any candid examination of their plight. But, though the '60s were plainly not all bad, it is hard to imagine that we would have experienced to the same degree such problems as family breakdown and fatherlessness, atomisation and loneliness, teenage pregnancy, widespread drug abuse, social exclusion, an abject lack of discipline in the education system, and the steady drip of lawlessness and disorder on our streets, if we had not chosen quite the path we did back then. Can anyone sincerely deny that we have reaped over the past half century what we sowed?

It was a couple of decades after the 1960s student protests that their protagonists – the *soixante-huitards*, as they came to be known – came of age and really started to put their stamp on politics and wider society. In particular, they established the beginnings of a cultural hegemony across the public sphere, particularly in the fields of education and law, and throughout our public services. They also began to wield greater clout in the national media.

Their influence was felt keenly across the mainstream British Left. Thus it was no coincidence that the ethos of the Labour Party and wider labour movement began to change around that time. Until then, Labour had remained anchored as a working-class party. There had long been middle-class liberals in it, of course – particularly among its higher echelons and leading thinkers – and it was always the better for that. It had also traditionally enjoyed the support of a layer of educated, professional and liberal middle-class voters. This was a necessary and finely balanced electoral compromise, and one which had broadly served the party well. The working class was generally willing to accept a modicum of social liberalism if it was introduced gradually, and provided the party continued to champion its economic interests. (So, for example, Labour governments of the 1960s and 1970s were able to introduce various liberal reforms, such as the abolition of the death penalty, without too much of a backlash from its core vote.)

But the greater part of that historical alliance had always been the working-class element – those who toiled for a living, the men and women of Britain's industrial heartlands, the workers and trade unionists employed in the shipyards, mines, steelworks, factories and offices of the nation, the families of moderate means living in council properties or, occasionally, fortunate enough to own their own modest homes. These millions, proud of their working-class heritage and imbued with a deep affinity for place and tradition, were the party's core vote, its base, its raison d'être.

During the 1980s, a new, emergent liberal class – personified by the likes of Peter Mandelson, Charles Clarke and Patricia Hewitt – began to secure key positions in the Labour Party as behind-the-scenes apparatchiks. As they did so, the bonds with the working class that had sustained the party for generations slowly, almost imperceptibly at first, started to weaken. A concerted effort to transform the image of Labour from an avowedly working-class 'cloth cap' party to one which embraced the new cosmopolitan liberalism was under way. The party was becoming centred around a new urban, modern, middle-class, internationalist and progressive style of politics. By the mid 1990s, Tony Blair, though he occasionally exhibited traces of a communitarian and Christian socialist style of politics, had become the ideal front man for the project. Needless to say, the BBC and liberal commentariat lapped it up.

These social and cultural revolutionaries who had taken control of the levers of power inside the party were disdainful of the early Labour tradition and the party's roots in Christian socialism and the trade union and co-operative movements. They frowned upon the quietly patriotic and socially conservative values to which so many in the party – from its working-class supporters to past leaders and statesmen – had held true. They saw no space for this 'faith, family and flag' nonsense in their shiny, new, socially liberal party. They elevated the cosmopolitan over the communitarian, the global over the local, the progressive over the conservative, modernity over tradition.

Their social and cultural radicalism was not matched, however, by any sort of economic radicalism. On the contrary, the Labour Party – or 'New Labour' as it became known during the Blair years – made its peace not only with the market itself but with the most severe strains of free-market ideology.

New Labour did little to challenge Thatcherite orthodoxy and, indeed, came to adopt many of the precepts of monetarist economics that had been the hallmark of Margaret Thatcher's reign. This meant forswearing any sort of radical economic programme or overt preference towards government intervention in the economy and, in their place, broadly accepting a framework centred on lighter-touch government, rolling back the frontiers of the state and allowing the market to dominate.

Thus, most of the restrictive trade union laws passed by the Tories in the 1980s remained in place, and there was no effort to reverse the privatisation and outsourcing of public services such as rail and energy. If anything, New Labour sought to open the door to greater involvement of private companies in the public sphere, with the internal marketisation of the National Health Service, the part-privatisation of the London Underground, an attempt (later abandoned) to part-privatise Royal Mail, and the expansion of the Private Finance Initiative. Income tax rates for the wealthiest remained low in comparison to many other European countries, and little effort was made to halt years of deindustrialisation, including the decline of manufacturing.

Asked in 2001 by the BBC's Jeremy Paxman whether the increase in the gap between rich and poor under his premiership was acceptable, Tony Blair went through all manner of contortions to avoid saying 'no', instead arguing – just as Thatcher did in response to such questions – that he had no desire to go after those with wealth, but instead wanted to 'level up' those at the bottom.[2] His stance echoed that of Peter Mandelson, who had famously declared in a speech to Silicon Valley executives in 1999 that New Labour was 'intensely relaxed about people getting filthy rich'.

This approach was at odds with nearly a century of Labour tradition, during which the belief in redistribution of wealth as a means to reducing inequality and creating a fairer society and greater opportunity for the less well-off was a cornerstone of party philosophy.

New Labour's first significant act upon coming to power in 1997 was to grant independence over monetary policy to the Bank of England. In so doing, it relinquished control of the money supply – a vital weapon in the armoury of any government – to bankers. It was a move entirely commensurate with its indulgence of the City and obsession with monetary targets over the needs of the real economy, where new wealth and jobs were created. It was market-driven Thatcherism – elevating restraint of inflation over growth and employment as macroeconomic policy goals – dressed in Labour clothes.

This represented a sharp departure from the attitude

of previous Labour governments, which had understood that their principal responsibility was to use every available lever to manage the economy in such a way as to enable them to build homes, create jobs and fund public services. Cumulatively, it revealed a party that was ultimately content to hand control of key functions – the running of public services and the management of central planks of economic policy – to business and technocrats.

Much of Blair and New Labour's economic philosophy was founded on the ideas of the sociologist Anthony Giddens, an advocate of the 'Third Way'. The Third Way approach sought to recognise – if not actively welcome – the reality of the new unrestrained globalised market, and saw the role of government as stretching to little beyond simply trying to give a leg up to those at the bottom of the ladder. This meant a broad acceptance that market-driven outcomes were the most desirable, and that the rich must be permitted to go on accruing increasingly eye-watering amounts of wealth just so long as the lot of the poor improved too.

Thus, while much effort was expended on raising the incomes of, and widening the opportunities for, the worse off – improvements for which New Labour deserves credit – the accelerating economic inequality was tolerated as the price to pay for demonstrating that the remodelled Labour Party was comfortable with the new capitalism. Blair's government did some good through introducing a national minimum wage, tax credits and investing in schools and hospitals, but ultimately the main tenets of Thatcher's monetarism remained in place under New Labour, albeit now with a more human face.

Blair himself saw limited scope for government intervention in a modern market economy, eschewing regulation other than where he considered it absolutely necessary. He had little interest in macroeconomic policy, nor any truck with the argument that a core responsibility of governments of the Left was to use every tool available to them, including both monetary and fiscal policy, to secure the best outcome for ordinary people. This hands-off attitude held even when the global financial crisis hit, shortly after Blair had left Downing Street. Writing later about the crisis, he opined: 'The role of government is to stabilise and then get out of the way as quickly as is economically sensible.'[3]

### Nowhere else to go?

All of these deep shifts on social and economic policy meant that, for many of its traditional supporters, the Labour Party felt less like the home it once did. It had become both socially and economically liberal when much of its core vote was the opposite. But New Labour calculated that these voters had nowhere else to go – and this was in large part true. In the first years after 1997, the Tories, under leaders such as William Hague and Iain Duncan Smith, were in such disarray that they presented no threat to Labour's hegemony. Moreover, for many people in the traditional Labour heartlands, such was the historical stigma attached to voting for the Conservatives – a party that had long been regarded as the enemy by swathes of the working class – it was always unlikely they would suddenly decide to throw their lot in with them. They understood that the nature of British politics had long been such that at each general election one of just two parties – Conservative or Labour – was likely to form the government, and they knew they would be better off under Labour, even if the party was increasingly becoming unrecognisable to them.

But as Labour slowly severed the umbilical cord linking it to the working class, large numbers of its once loyal voters, feeling unwanted, began to abstain in elections or flock to UKIP. Some were even attracted by the far-right British National Party, which – by tapping into voter concerns over immigration and seeking to cloak its racism in the language of identity, patriotism, community and tradition – began to gain ground in areas with sizeable white working-class populations, helping it to win a seat on the London Assembly in 2008 and two at the European Parliament elections in 2009, with 6.3 per cent of the vote.

Labour lost a third of its vote (5 million in total) between the 1997 and 2010 general elections. In this period, the party haemorrhaged support from the C2DE social grade (occupational working class). At the 1997 general election, 59 per cent of Labour votes came from the C2DEs and 41 per cent from the ABC1s (occupational middle class). In 2010, for the first time, Labour won more votes from the ABC1s than it did the C2DEs.[4] That Britain itself had become more middle class during these years provides only a partial explanation for this phenomenon.

Any hope that a Jeremy Corbyn leadership would rekindle the relationship between the Labour Party and the working class proved to be deeply misplaced. In many respects, the situation worsened under Corbyn. While the Labour vote increased both as a share and in absolute terms at the 2017 general election, the evidence shows that the middle class swung to Labour and the working class to the Tories.[5] In particular, the Conservatives won more votes than Labour among the C2DEs.[6]

And then the 2019 general election brought Labour its worst result since 1935, with so-called Red Wall seats tumbling all over the place and the Tories securing the votes of 48 per cent of C2DEs compared to Labour's 33 per cent.[7] That Labour could perform so dismally at the ballot box after the Tories had for a decade imposed a programme of grinding austerity – the brunt of which was borne by the poorest – throws into even sharper relief the extent of the breach between the party and its traditional base.

While it is true that Labour under Corbyn rejected much of the neoliberalism of New Labour and pursued an economic policy more favourable to the party's traditional supporters, what the outcome of the 2017 and 2019 elections showed was that the promise of economic justice alone wasn't enough. Working-class voters yearned for something more.

The Labour membership data illustrates yet further the degree to which the party has moved away from the working class. A survey of Labour members conducted in 2017 found that 77 per cent fell within the ABC1 grade, nearly half of all the party's members lived in London or southern England, and 57 per cent were graduates.[8]

Peter Hyman, chief speechwriter and strategist for Tony Blair when he was prime minister, wrote illuminatingly in 2015:

New Labour sought political hegemony: winning power and locking out the Tories to ensure that the 21st century was a Labour century with Labour values in contrast to a Tory-dominated 20th century. The scale of that ambition, in a country dominated by a stridently Right-wing press and the quiet conservatism of large swathes of the British people, was breathtaking.[9]

What Hyman – and New Labour generally – fatally misunderstood was that those 'large swathes' of the population imbued with that 'quiet conservatism' included many traditional Labour voters living in the party's working-class heartlands.

Hyman's words mirrored those of Blair himself in a speech to the Labour Party conference in 1999, in which he railed against Britain's 'forces of conservatism', attacking not just the Conservative Party but small 'c' conservatism of any kind, whether social, moral or cultural. Labour's 'new radicals' would 'set the people free', Blair promised. The 'forces of conservatism' were responsible for 'the old prejudices, where foreign means bad'. They had 'kept people down' and 'stunted people's potential'. They were, according to Blair, the reason Martin Luther King was dead and Nelson Mandela 'spent the best years of his life in a cell the size of a bed'.

As well as being a rather unpleasant mix of hyperbole and caricature, the speech represented a thorough repudiation of much of Britain's history and tradition. Blair displayed not the slightest recognition, as he set us on this path to his brave new world, that these forces of conservatism might have been right on anything at all, or that his own party's supporters might actually have some affinity for that history and tradition.

Blair developed these themes in his address to the 2005 Labour conference, telling delegates:

> I hear people say we have to stop and debate globalisation. You might as well debate whether autumn should follow summer . . . The character of this changing world is indifferent to tradition. Unforgiving of frailty. No respecter of past reputations. It has no custom and practice. It is replete with opportunities, but they only go to those swift to adapt, slow to complain, open, willing and able to change.

He may as well have said: 'There is no such thing as society, only money and trade.' The global market was supreme; history had nothing to teach us; the future was liberal and progressive; the nation state should resign itself to its growing irrelevance; any affection for tradition would only serve to hold us back; don't harbour silly notions of social stability or attachment to place; shape up or ship out. That was Blair's message.

The effect of Labour's transformation over the past thirty years into a far more liberal, urban, middle-class, globalist party is that it has been largely hollowed out of working-class representation and influence, with increasingly fewer individuals from working-class backgrounds representing it at the highest levels.

The party neither looks nor sounds very much like those it was created to represent. Many of its representatives and spokespeople – indeed, much of its membership – live wholly different lives, and have contrasting interests and priorities, to millions of working-class people living in the more disadvantaged parts of our nation.

Let us take as a hypothetical example a person from a working-class background living in a post-industrial town. They may once have been employed as a manual worker and seen their industry disintegrate as – thanks to globalisation – production was outsourced overseas. Or they may have suffered from downward pressure on their wages and seen an increased strain on local services as a result of mass immigration. Their hometown would have experienced a lack of decent employment, housing and opportunity. This person might have expected a Labour government to have fought their corner; to have developed a credible industrial strategy designed to halt the process of deindustrialisation and create the kind of sustainable blue-collar jobs upon which so many families in such places relied; to build the necessary number of council houses; to regulate the labour supply so as to protect wages; to breathe new life into their town rather than accept its industrial decline as a consequence of the new global market.

The chances are that this hypothetical person would hold what some might regard as old-fashioned views on certain social issues. They might, for instance, be a practising Roman Catholic or vaguely religious in some other way. They might respect other faiths, but believe that Christianity, as the rock upon which so much of our nation's heritage, law and morality were built, should be prioritised over them. They might be tolerant and understanding towards gay and lesbian people, but believe that marriage should ultimately be between a man and woman. They might feel compassion towards those experiencing an unwanted pregnancy, but believe abortion to be wrong. They might be sympathetic to the challenges experienced by single parents, but consider the rise in divorce rates and fatherlessness to have been catastrophic – and they might expect society to be confident about saying so. They might defend the right of individuals to live, dress and worship as they please, but believe state-sponsored multiculturalism to have undermined the cohesion and unity of communities. They might be kind and welcoming to migrants, but feel unease at the way in which mass immigration has fundamentally – and so rapidly – altered our communities and way of life. They might be patriotic without being nationalistic or xenophobic. They might consider crime to be a vice worthy of punishment, not a disease deserving of treatment, and that those who commit heinous murder should not be allowed to live out their natural lives. They might believe that a welfare system should be rooted in the concepts of reciprocity and conditionality rather than absolute entitlement. They might hold to the view that a person with a penis cannot be a woman. They might believe that the authorities should do more to prevent the widespread use of illegal drugs, rather than routinely turning a blind eye to it.

One isn't required to subscribe to all – or indeed any – of these views personally to recognise that millions of working-class voters in today's Britain still hold them, as indeed they do other such values centred around nation, family, tradition, morality and place. And here's the thing: there was a time when the Labour Party was the natural home for these people. They voted for it – as did their parents and grandparents before them – because it represented people like themselves. It wasn't just for reasons of self-interest; often it was tribal. Labour was the party of the working class and trade unions. It spoke for them and was proud to have them in its ranks. It was rooted in their communities, and often they would join or campaign for it. They were its backbone.

But so many of these millions look at today's Labour Party – replete with its middle-class, *Guardian*-reading bohemians and pseudo-intellectuals, and pursuing an uber-liberal, youth-obsessed, London-centric agenda – and feel unwanted. Today's Labour Party treats them as if they were an embarrassing elderly relative. It still wants their votes, but it doesn't want to be seen in public with them. Their views are antediluvian and reactionary. They haven't caught up with the liberal political enlightenment. One can only wonder how past Labour heavyweights such as Clement Attlee and Ernest Bevin, old-fashioned patriots to their fingertips, would fare in today's party.

The aversion felt by many inside Labour towards working-class voters – and vice versa – was summed up by Suzy Stride, who stood as the party's candidate in the marginal constituency of Harlow in Essex at the 2015 general election. Harlow was a post-war new town which became home to thousands of aspiring Londoners who had escaped the overcrowding of the capital. With a large working-class population, it is regularly depicted as the home of 'White Van Man'. Writing after the election, Stride said of Harlow: 'A strong sense of civic pride resulted from the sense of a community that people had (sometimes quite literally) built together.'

She recalled that:

> the most frequent thing people said to us on the doorstep was 'You're all the same'. Increasingly as time went on, we realised that 'You're all the same' really meant 'You're nothing like me' or 'You know nothing about my life' – and to an extent they were right.

She was caustic in her assessment of how voters in the town perceived Labour Party campaigners.

> Among our activist base, manual workers were small in number, and increasingly the Labour Party was viewed like middle-class Ryanair passengers having to stomach a couple of hours' flight with people they shared little in common with; it could be uncomfortable, but it got you where you needed to go.

She concluded that:

> Labour has always existed as a coalition of middle-class, ideological socialists and social democrats and pragmatic working people working to improve their circumstances through collective endeavour. In Harlow it was clear that people thought that this coalition had become unbalanced.[10]

Stride failed to win the seat.

The name Gillian Duffy is enough to make most Labour Party activists break out in a cold sweat. Her encounter with the then prime minister Gordon Brown during his visit to Rochdale in the 2010 general election gave the starkest illustration of the gulf between the modern Labour Party and its one-time core support. Duffy, a pensioner and lifelong Labour voter, challenged Brown – in not especially intemperate terms – over the impact of mass immigration into her community. After their exchange, Brown was picked up on a TV microphone referring to her as a 'bigoted woman'. He said it because he believed it, albeit he later apologised. And in saying it, he was exhibiting publicly the private contempt that so many in the Labour Party felt towards people such as Mrs Duffy.

Then there was Emily Thornberry. While campaigning for Labour in the Rochester and Strood by-election in 2014, she tweeted a photo of a house adorned with St George flags, outside which a white van was parked. 'Image from Rochester' was the caption she chose to post alongside the photo. The tweet generated a media storm. Thornberry, the MP for Islington South – heart of liberal elite country – stood accused of demonstrating a sneering mockery towards working-class voters and of harbouring the belief that such displays of patriotism were distasteful. She was forced to resign her shadow cabinet role as Attorney General. Like Brown before her, she had made the error of making her private antipathy public. The episode prompted Labour's candidate in that by-election, Naushabah Khan, to say: 'In one image, Labour had almost destroyed its foundations, displaying a growing detachment from our roots.'[11]

The journalist and commentator David Goodhart – a one-time fully paid-up member of the liberal class who found himself ostracised by friends in his north London tribe when he began to question the wisdom of mass immigration – dissected this schism in his book *The Road to Somewhere*.[12] Goodhart posited that

Britain is divided between those who see the world from 'Anywhere' – mobile, more educated and affluent, less attached to place, imbued with a liberal worldview – and those who see it from 'Somewhere' – poorer, less educated, more rooted, and with a greater sense of cultural attachment. Until recently, Anywheres were a relatively small group. But now they make up around a quarter of the population. The Somewheres comprise around half, with the rest 'inbetweeners'.

Despite their inferior numbers, however, the Anywheres dominate our politics and culture. This, argues Goodhart, often leads them to believe they are governing in the national interest when in fact they are governing in the Anywhere interest. Thus, for example, Anywheres, with their support for economic and cultural openness, and because they are able to take advantage of it, are more likely to support EU free movement; whereas Somewheres, with few or no escape routes and often already suffering the effects of low pay, are more apt to experience its negative side effects and therefore more likely to oppose it. Yet still so much of the political class sees free movement as an inherently good thing.

Jon Cruddas, one-time political secretary to Tony Blair and now the MP for Dagenham and Rainham, has articulated the pressing need for Labour to understand the patriotism of working-class communities such as the one he represents, and to embrace a 'modern, radical Englishness'.[13] According to Cruddas, New Labour became all about the 'progressive new': 'People in this country . . . are fearful for their jobs, their families and their communities, as they experience the most destructive period of capitalism since the 1930s. They yearn to fight against their insecurity. But how do you resist when all the political parties are progressive?' Channelling George Orwell, Cruddas concludes: 'This is why we need an English socialism that resists relentless commodification, values the land, believes in family life, takes pride in the country and its traditions: a conservative socialism.'[14]

Cruddas is right to assert that all the main political parties – even the Tories – have adopted the progressive agenda. That's why it would be wrong to characterise liberal progressivism as a philosophy that exists only on the Left (though that is certainly where it has always sat most comfortably). David Cameron was able to win the Tory leadership in 2005 by presenting himself as a modern progressive – allegedly describing himself during that contest as the 'heir to Blair' – and later formed a coalition government with the ultra-progressive Liberal Democrats with little kickback from his own party.

No major UK party can be said today to genuinely exhibit much more than a trace of a socially conservative agenda. Theresa May, upon being elected to lead the Conservative Party in 2016, did attempt to appeal to voters in Labour's traditional working-class heartlands by leaning towards a more communitarian approach – in her first conference speech as leader she famously said, 'If you believe you are a citizen of the world, you are a citizen of nowhere' – but this was soon abandoned. And while the Tories under Boris Johnson have again pitched towards these communities – reaping the dividends at the 2019 general election – it would be wrong to portray this more widely as a departure from the dominant socially liberal and progressive doctrine. All the major parties have broadly embraced the 'Anywhere' programme of radical social and cultural liberalism. 'Somewheres' and their priorities are indulged only to a point.

Footage of its past annual conferences reveals the extent to which the Labour Party in particular has been transformed. As recently as the 1990s, the conference hall was populated by a sizeable number of working-class MPs and delegates from local parties and the trade unions. These were often people who had worked in manual jobs and were rooted in the old industrial heart-lands. An array of accents would be heard from the rostrum and beyond.

These days – and I attend the conference in person every year, so know this – the demographic has changed dramatically. Those with any background rooted in the old industrial working class are increasingly a rarity – museum pieces among the ranks of middle-class liberals and crypto-Marxists who now fill the conference hall and fringe. Most of the party's activists and members are separated by a social and cultural chasm from its traditional working-class base.

Many commentators, including some from within the party, attributed this divide in more recent times to the leadership of Jeremy Corbyn. Some of them have argued that only by readopting a Blairite centrist agenda would Labour reconnect with the broad mass of the electorate, including working-class communities. But this is wrong-headed, not least because it ignores the reality that it was this agenda that ultimately did so much to alienate working-class voters from the party in the first place. Corbyn had many faults, but only the wilfully blind could conclude that the malaise set in only after his election as leader. Anyone who believes that a return to centrism would revitalise the Labour Party would do well to consider the fate of 'Change UK', the breakaway organisation founded by anti-Brexit MPs on Blairite principles of liberal and progressive internationalism, but which swiftly sank without trace.

The very term 'centrist' is, of course, designed to give the impression of sensible moderation, a position held by wise and reasonable heads to which only those on the extremes do not subscribe. In fact, the self-described centrists are often the most strident of ideologues, pursuing a militantly liberal agenda and only too willing to trash centuries of tradition and custom. Far from being the voices of 'mainstream common sense', in reality theirs is a worldview completely at odds with the beliefs of millions. The truth is that the 'centre ground', in so far as it exists at all, shifts over time, and what passes for conventional wisdom among the elite at one point in time may not do so at another.

But while Labour under Corbyn was arguably more attuned to the demand among working-class voters for a fairer and more egalitarian economy, it made no progress at all on closing the cultural divide. Those advocating a return to a communitarian politics built around the centrality of place, belonging, family, vocation, patriotism and reciprocity are vanishingly small in number inside today's Labour Party. Though theirs is a tradition that can be traced back to the early days of Labour – emerging from a rich working-class culture of local democracy and participation in civic institutions, trade unions, co-operatives, mutuals and the like – it is now a fringe tendency, overwhelmed by the mass of middle-class members, activists and party representatives wedded to a more cosmopolitan liberal outlook.

Of course, we are invited to believe that the liberal left and far-left factions that wield so much influence in today's Labour Party are sworn enemies, separated by an ideological chasm. But in many respects the war between the sides, both of which are heavily populated by the metropolitan middle classes, is a phoney one. Sure, there are differences, such as on economic and foreign policy. But the social policy of both groups is anchored in their shared bourgeois, liberal, cosmopolitan, progressive, globalist worldview, meaning that they have far more in common than either would care to admit.

In these times, the traditional working class cannot even look to the trade union movement for succour. Historically, the Trades Union Congress (TUC) and the leadership of the big unions were the proud voice of industrial Britain. The unions were hugely influential throughout private industry and part of the lifeblood of our working-class heartlands. But now they are virtually absent from these industries and communities. This is, of course, in no small measure due to the double whammy of anti-trade-union legislation and deindustrialisation which the trade union movement found itself confronting in the 1980s, and from which it has never fully recovered. But it is also a consequence of the movement's decision, in response to those challenges, to retreat to its public sector comfort zone – the most recent figures show that 3.7 million union members, 58 per cent of the total, work in the public sector,[15] despite only 17 per cent of workers overall being employed there[16] – and to become effectively a mouthpiece for the liberal class. Thus the TUC and a number of unions are now preoccupied with promoting identity politics over class politics, and regularly formulate policy to accord with their liberal, and often very London-centric, ideology. This, partly, is what drove them to campaign for Remain in the EU referendum, and then to come out in support of a second referendum when Leave won. (It is worth noting here the contrast with the 1975 referendum on Common Market membership, when a majority of trade unions wanted to leave.[17])

None of this comes as much of a surprise to those of us rooted in the movement who have witnessed its transformation over recent years, and in particular the emergence of a new brand of trade union official and policy-maker arriving at the top, not after having worked for many years on the shop floor or as a workplace rep, but carried on the conveyor belt taking them from university into policy and research departments and then into leading positions.

The tragedy is that with the advent of such things as the gig economy, sweatshop warehouses and the growth in precarious and transient employment, including the rise of zero-hours contracts, trade unions are needed in private industry as much as ever. But, by and large, they aren't there. And the movement has no serious strategy to remedy the situation.

To the working class, then, it must seem that both their political and industrial representatives have failed them. Worse, those representatives are often openly contemptuous of them.

The strand within the labour movement that was imbued with socially conservative, patriotic, communitarian values has now been almost expunged from it. And when it decided to abandon this tradition, the movement turned many working-class voters away from political engagement or, worse, made them prey to the forces of the populist Right.

### The Brexit revolt

All of which brings us back to the EU referendum. The vote to leave was not the cause of our nation's polarisation; it was a symptom of it. Brexit was the manifestation of revenge on the part of a long-neglected section of society. Millions who had witnessed their beliefs and values ignored or scorned by an arrogant liberal establishment had suddenly been handed a weapon with which to hit back. They saw that the referendum crossed party boundaries, and thus felt released from normal tribal loyalties. Those who had voted Labour all their lives observed that some Labour MPs, albeit a small number, and other activists from the Left were supporting the Leave campaign while much of the Tory Party and big business were supporting Remain, and concluded that they could vote Leave without being accused of lining up with their historical political enemies.

They understood, too, that a vote to leave would send a shockwave through the entire establishment, and calculated that this was a thing worth doing if it forced their political masters to finally sit up and take notice of them. It was therefore no surprise that, upon being presented with such an opportunity, so many – including large numbers who had never voted in their lives – decided to take it.

In this context, it would be wrong to characterise the Leave vote as one which was motivated solely by antipathy towards the European Union, less still by any sort of hostility towards Europe the continent. Undoubtedly those who voted for Brexit did wish for the UK to leave the EU. Evidence shows that the desire for self-government and sovereignty, for control over immigration and for the reassertion of democracy over the rule of unelected technocrats were all big drivers in the decision of Leave voters.[18]

However, Brexit should also be seen as a blow struck by a brooding and resentful electorate against the British ruling class as well as the EU elite. With a referendum looming, an establishment which had abandoned and forgotten so many of its own citizens was suddenly demanding their solidarity in this most crucial of votes. The main political parties, big business, the banking industry – all these people and institutions who were, as Leave voters saw it, mainly responsible for their plight, for the hardship and privations and sense of loss they had experienced – were now desperate for their support. Little surprise that they weren't inclined to lend it. As the writer and ethnographer Lisa Mckenzie argued:

> For some working-class people in the UK – those who had experienced political, economic and social exclusion – the question they saw on the ballot paper was not about leaving or remaining in the European Union, but was 'Do you want things to stay the same, or do you want things to be different?' Those people . . . answered. They wanted things to change; they wanted things to be different.[19]

The dire warnings issued during the campaign about what would likely happen in the event of a Leave vote appeared, if anything, to have the opposite effect to that intended. The scaremongering was cranked up to epic proportions by the establishment. There was the threat of an immediate recession and an emergency austerity budget, galloping inflation and interest rates, rocketing unemployment, even the suggestion that peace in Europe would be in peril. But it served only to solidify the position of prospective Leave voters.

The prophecies of disaster failed to hit home for three reasons. First, they were so blatantly overhyped, and in being so lost much of their impact. (As we now know, none of the worst forecasts of doom came to pass following the Leave vote.) Second, predictions of economic meltdown had little resonance among those for whom the economy had, in any case, long ago stopped working, and who felt therefore they had little to lose from disrupting the prevailing economic order. Third, Leave voters calculated that the referendum might be the only opportunity they would be handed in their lifetime to force the political elite to listen to them. Their votes were taken for granted in general elections, such that few saw these elections as a chance to effect real change, and certainly not change on the scale that a vote to leave the European Union would precipitate. But with the referendum they had been handed a gun with one bullet, and they felt obliged to use it, no matter the political or economic fall-out.

Even so, Brexit should be seen as rooted in much more than a simple desire by Leave voters to inflict a well-deserved bloody nose on their British and EU rulers. For many Leave voters, Brexit was always a long-term project. It was an opportunity to shake-up the entire system, to trigger a radical realignment of political and economic priorities. To vote Leave was their way of saying, 'Hey, what about us?', a reminder from the forgotten millions to the elites that they still had the power, through the ballot box, to challenge the status quo, to disturb their cosy club, to drag them back to first principles and make them start again.

In this respect – and I say this as someone who has taken strike action on several occasions – Brexit can be viewed as something akin to a vote by workers for a strike. As with workers who vote for strike action, Leave voters knew their vote would create turbulence and disrupt operations; they knew that they would likely be attacked for it; and some may have even believed they would take a hit financially, at least in the immediate aftermath of the vote. But for them it was a case of short-term pain for potential long-term gain. They were willing to take the risk of losing out financially if it helped to deliver something better in the future. 'The bosses have stopped listening to us. Everybody out.' It was, as it nearly always is for workers taking strike action, a last resort when everything else had failed.

And for those of us who campaigned for Leave from a Left perspective, there was the added factor that we considered the EU to be an explicitly anti-socialist institution which elevated the demands of the market above all else, embedded austerity and deflationary economics, restricted state aid to industry, enshrined laws designed to militate against public ownership and investment, and had caused widespread unemployment. In this, we stood in the tradition of past luminaries of the labour movement such as Tony Benn, Michael Foot, Peter Shore, Barbara Castle and Bob Crow.

In fact, the Left's volte-face from EU-scepticism to something approaching EU-fanaticism is one of the talking points of modern politics. The former, once mainstream inside the labour movement, is now a minority position. Support for EU membership has become an article of faith among Labour MPs, activists and trade union leaders, with Brexit routinely – and fallaciously – denounced as a 'right-wing project'.

This shift, whose origins can be traced to the late 1980s, resulted from a chronic loss of confidence among the movement's leaders. Cowed by Margaret Thatcher's offensive against the unions, which included the defeat of the miners, they turned to the EU for deliverance. They bought the myth of a 'workers' Europe', sold to them by the EU's left-leaning bureaucrats such as Jacques Delors. They opted, as Tony Benn put it, for the good king over the bad parliament. The anti-democratic capitalist club was suddenly a beacon of social and economic progress. Except it wasn't. Because neoliberal economics and an aversion to democracy remained hard-wired in the EU.

The Left's failure, before and after the referendum, to properly reflect the concerns of the millions in working-class heartlands who voted Leave served to widen the gulf between it and them. Labour activists comforted themselves with the knowledge that a majority of Labour supporters voted Remain. But this ignored the reality that the party, if it was to regain power, could not rely only on its existing vote, but needed to move heaven and earth to recapture the votes of the millions who had deserted it over previous years. One startling statistic among many is that among those who abstained from voting in the 2015 general election, Leave commanded a sixteen-point lead.[20]

Rather than embrace Brexit and recognise it for what it was – a fundamental rejection of the status quo and an opportunity for an incoming Labour government to reorder the UK economy free from the shackles of the EU – labour movement figures publicly railed against it from the outset, often joining forces with business leaders in their resistance. It smacked of a Left that had taken the side of the establishment over the people.

I saw this attitude up close when I was present in the hall during a debate on Brexit at the 2018 Labour Party conference in Liverpool. A young delegate from Blyth Valley in Northumberland – a working-class constituency which voted Leave in large numbers – urged the conference not to support a second referendum. He spoke passionately of how free movement and deindustrialisation had afflicted his community, and warned that Labour was in danger of losing the support of his fellow constituents. Though his words attracted a smattering of applause, there were – in the section where I was sat, at least – plenty of boos and catcalls too. They didn't want to hear it.

At the 2019 general election, Blyth Valley returned a Conservative MP for the first time in its history.

On 29 March 2019, I spoke at a rally for democracy in Parliament Square. It was two years to the day since Article 50 had been triggered and thus should have been the day on which the UK left the EU. But Theresa

May and her government had begged for – and secured – an extension. Thousands came to the rally from all parts of the UK to express their displeasure and demand that politicians respect their vote and implement Brexit. The event had the distinct whiff of a genuine grassroots rebellion against the system. Some of those present had never been to a demonstration in their lives.

It ought to have been fertile territory for the Left. These angry, disenfranchised voters – many of them from ordinary working-class backgrounds and communities – were fighting back against the establishment's efforts to undermine democracy and silence their voices. It rarely gets more serious.

But while some individual trade unionists and Labour voters joined the throng, the official Left was conspicuous by its absence. The Labour Party and trade unions, which should have been there in force, were nowhere to be seen. No general secretaries. No banners. No placards. Just a solitary Labour MP. It was both a missed opportunity and a sad indictment of how the Left was no longer willing to speak for the working class.

Not that Brexit in itself is the answer to all our problems, of course. Leaving the EU should not, even by those of us who supported it, be seen a panacea for the challenges confronting working-class people. It is instead merely a means to an end – a necessary but insufficient step, if you will.

The real problems created by austerity, globalisation, deindustrialisation, precarious employment and lack of trade union representation won't disappear immediately we become a self-governing country again. But what Brexit will do is restore our national democracy and free us – and, more pertinently, a future radical Labour government – from the straitjacket of the neoliberal EU's regulations and directives. Brexit therefore represents at least an opportunity to clear a path to a different future. Socialism before Brexit is impossible. It must be the other way round.

It became clear in the period after the referendum that neither the Left nor much of the wider establishment had learned any lessons from the vote. These elements deployed all sorts of shabby tactics designed to thwart the implementation of the people's decision. In the context of the imbalance in support for Brexit between the people and their representatives, this was perhaps not surprising: an estimated 64 per cent of constituencies in Britain voted Leave in the referendum,[21] yet just 159 of 650 MPs did the same.[22] And for all the subsequent bluster from some MPs about how the vote was 'rigged', how Brexit was always going to be impossible, how the question on the ballot paper was too simplistic and so on, it's worth remembering that five out of six of them voted to hold the referendum, and many of these had spoken of the need to respect the outcome, whatever it was. It can only be presumed that they did so because they didn't for a moment think they would lose.

It became plain almost immediately after the vote that politicians and the Westminster commentariat had not quite grasped what had happened, or why it had happened. The discussion among them became fixed on the dry, technical aspects of Brexit: the merits or otherwise of the Single Market and Customs Union, the Irish border and so on. Whereas the issues that actually drove so many to vote Leave – community, place, identity, democracy, self-government, belonging – were largely ignored in the post-referendum debate.

Desperate to deflect any suggestion that entrenched liberal dogma might be responsible for the sense of anger and displacement felt by millions, prominent opponents of Brexit sought to blame everything and everyone but themselves: 'fake news', slogans on buses, Russian bots, Arron Banks, Cambridge data firms, and suchlike. They resorted to the worst kind of paternalistic arguments in their efforts to derail Brexit. Leave voters heard many times that they 'didn't know what they were voting for' and had been conned by propaganda and lies. At the extreme, they were labelled as 'thick', 'racist' and 'gammon'.

It felt at times as if Britain had regressed to the Victorian era, when working-class people were told they weren't worthy of the vote because they couldn't be trusted with it.

### Liberals versus the masses

The contempt in which some within the liberal establishment and intelligentsia appeared to hold the principle of democracy in the weeks and months after the referendum was striking. One can't help but conclude that many of them would be happier to see the world run by technocrats of the 'right' persuasion. Take, for example, these words spoken by the novelist and journalist Howard Jacobson in an interview in 2018: 'We're coming to the comeuppance of democracy. You can't trust the people . . . you can be certain that the people will get it wrong. They'd already done it, as far as I was concerned, in Brexit . . . And then with Trump again. The people given this new confidence in their own opinions. Their inability to distinguish true from false.'[23]

Other members of the political and cultural elites seemed to be trying to outdo each other in their displays of hysteria and contempt for the masses. Examples include Labour MP David Lammy speaking of 'the will of the people bollocks'[24] and suggesting that a pro-Brexit

47

group of Tory MPs were modern-day Nazis;[25] *Guardian* columnist Polly Toynbee claiming in January 2019 that the UK was now a 'Remainer' nation as 'more young remainers joined the electoral register' and 'more old leavers died' (she went on: 'A Final Say vote would stop the will of the dead ruling over the will of the young');[26] Lord Adonis referring to those attempting to thwart Brexit as 'the resistance';[27] Liberal Democrat leader Vince Cable stating that Brexit represented a backlash from old people who were 'driven by a nostalgia for a world where passports were blue, faces were white and the map was coloured imperial pink';[28] and Labour MP Barry Sheerman citing the fact that better-educated people voted Remain as evidence of the rightness of the Remain cause.[29]

In February 2019, a petition demanding the revocation of Article 50 was launched. It received backing from many celebrities, including the actor Hugh Grant, who implied that anyone unwilling to sign it was not 'sane'.[30] As if to underscore the divide between the UK's metropolitan areas and provinces, a 'heat map' showed the largest number of signatures came from university cities such as Bristol, Brighton, Cambridge, Edinburgh, Oxford and, naturally, London.[31]

Speaking on the BBC's *Politics Live* programme in 2019, author and *Guardian* contributor Will Self remarked, 'Every racist and anti-Semite in the country, pretty much, probably voted for Brexit.' When rebuked and asked by a fellow guest to apologise, Self retorted, 'To who? To racists and anti-Semites?' It was a classic guilt-by-association smear. One might just as well argue that, as all English racists support England in the World Cup, any non-racist who also supports England is tainted.

Then there was Professor Richard Dawkins, who,

while taking part in a march demanding a second referendum, tweeted:

> Yes of COURSE there are people who voted Leave for reasons other than xenophobic bigotry or fading imperial jingoism. I've met at least four. But it felt good to be marching through London with the hundred thousand yesterday. And to be reminded of the decent half of Britain.[32]

In other words, the other half was comprised of indecent bigots and those longing for the days of Empire.

These disingenuous efforts by the intelligentsia to portray the Leave vote as the will only of old, xenophobic white folk seeking to resurrect an imperial past is a lazy caricature which conflicts with the evidence. In fact, research shows that around a third of black and minority ethnic voters supported Leave,[33] and many of these were themselves hostile to EU free movement laws because they considered it unfair that prospective migrants from outside the union – often people like themselves – were placed at a disadvantage.[34]

Among Sikhs and Jews, Leave won majority support,[35] as it did in some areas – such as Luton, Birmingham, Bradford and Slough – with large minority ethnic populations. I think of my own in-laws, Anglo-Indians who arrived on a plane from Calcutta in the 1960s. Most of these in-laws voted for Brexit – and for precisely the same reasons as many white working-class voters did: the country they had settled in and grown fond of was slowly vanishing, and they felt little affinity with – and were uneasy at the increasing power of – the European Union.

The liberal commentariat struggles to get its head around such realities. Witness prominent journalist and TV presenter Robert Peston describing a referendum

campaign trip to Leicester: 'I assumed it was a collective wind-up when almost every Asian I met said
to me that they would be voting for Brexit, in part
because of their concerns about what they perceived
to be excessive immigration.'[36] Anything that didn't fit
with the caricature of Leave voters as knuckle-dragging
ethno-nationalists appeared to induce a sense of disorientation within some among our media and political
classes.

This crude demonisation of Brexit supporters surely
explains why, in the face of a scare campaign on an
unprecedented scale and a concerted effort to make
them think again, there was, in the period after the referendum, no conspicuous shift in public opinion. Over 17
million people voted Leave because they felt the political
establishment had stopped listening to them. And much
of that same establishment then set about doing everything it could to prove them right.

History will record Brexit as a genuine democratic
revolt by the working class, particularly the English
working class. Evidence shows that nearly two-thirds of
C2DEs voted Leave.[37] As professors Matthew Goodwin
and Oliver Heath explained:

> Many local authorities that recorded some of the strong-
> est support for Brexit are struggling areas where average
> incomes, education and skill levels are low and there are
> few opportunities to get ahead. Authorities that recorded
> some of the highest levels of support for Brexit include
> the working-class communities of Castle Point, Great
> Yarmouth, Mansfield, Ashfield, Stoke-on-Trent and
> Doncaster. In such communities, the types of opportuni-
> ties and life experiences contrast sharply with those in
> areas that are filled with more affluent, highly-educated,
> and diverse populations, which gave some of the strong-
> est support to remaining in the EU, such as Islington,

Edinburgh, Cambridge, Oxford and Richmond upon Thames.[38]

Moreover, a report by the Centre for Social Justice and Legatum Institute found that:

> At every level of earning there is a direct correlation between household income and your likelihood to vote for leaving the EU – 62 per cent of those with income of less than £20,000 voted to leave, but that percentage falls in steady increments until, by an income of £60,000, that percentage was just 35 per cent.[39]

That said, it would be a mistake to assume that only working-class voters in Britain are angry. In fact, it could be argued that there exists in our country today a new coalition – though one entirely accidental and uncoordinated – between, on the one hand, those once-loyal Labour voters in the party's old working-class heartlands and, on the other, middle-class Conservative voters in the shires and suburbs. These groups, long derided and neglected by the establishments of their respective parties on account of their traditional, 'unfashionable' views, feel alienated and resentful. It was an alliance that manifested itself most starkly in those millions of Leave votes in the referendum.

This unintended coalition has been likened by David Goodhart to the BBC sitcom *Gavin and Stacey*,[40] in which Gavin, from an aspiring middle-class family in suburban Essex, falls in love with Stacey, who hails from post-industrial south Wales. Their blossoming relationship, which ended in marriage, seems like a metaphor for the unlikely concord that has developed between the millions from both orbits who felt unrepresented in British politics over recent times.

An oft-repeated refrain from the EU enthusiasts, including Labour MPs, in justification of their efforts to block

Brexit was: 'No one voted to be poorer.' Aside from the fact that this presupposes that Britain *will* be poorer as a fully independent nation – a much-contested claim in itself – how can these people be sure they are correct? How do they know for certain that Leave voters weren't willing to trade a bit of personal wealth (such as they possessed any) in return for restoring the ability of the country to govern itself and regain control of its money, laws and borders, as well as raising the hope of rekindling a lost spirit of community, identity and belonging?

While it is true that there often exists among working-class voters a strong desire for self-advancement – which explains why, for example, many chose to buy their council homes when government reforms allowed them to do so – it does them the gravest disservice to imply that they are motivated solely or even predominantly by an economic imperative or self-interest. And those on the Left who resort to such arguments seem not to realise that they are in fact peddling pure market-obsessed Thatcherism: that it is 'all about the economy'; that quality-of-life factors are secondary to the need to make a fast buck; and that consideration for GDP figures must be elevated above any general desire for contentment.

Indeed, a poll carried out more than two years after the referendum, while a withdrawal agreement between the UK and EU was still being negotiated, showed that 66 per cent of those who had voted Leave said the government's priority for any deal should be leaving the EU and ending free movement completely – even if it meant causing disruption to the economy.[41]

Financial advancement isn't the be all and end all in traditional working-class communities, and never has been. These are communities that place a high value on social solidarity, cohesion and order. People on the Left who believe that, in the minds of those who populate these communities, such things are secondary to naked financial self-interest will be shocked to discover that the reverse is in fact true. By contrast, those who have been paying attention to what has been occurring in our country over the past thirty years were not at all surprised by the upheavals and divisions that broke out. They had been long in the making.

Because, in the end, a nation whose political and cultural elites spend years ignoring working-class concerns – elites who hitch their wagons to the causes of neo-liberalism and globalisation; who do little to intervene as factories close, entire industries disappear and an inestimable number of solid blue-collar jobs are transferred overseas; who preside over a social and cultural revolution while painting all those who express any opposition as narrow-minded bigots; who demonise millions of their fellow citizens who still hold true to traditional values; who degrade the concepts of patriotism and nationhood, insisting that open borders are universally beneficial no matter the social and economic disruption they cause; and who only ever speak to the working class about the things they want to speak about and not the things it wants to speak about – will, as sure as night follows day, be inviting a rebellion.

And just as such a rebellion erupted – and for broadly similar reasons – in the US Rust Belt with the election of Donald Trump, in provincial France with the Gilet Jaunes protests, and throughout much of Europe with the upsurge in populist movements, so too did it erupt in working-class Britain.

In a survey carried out by the ComRes polling organisation in March 2019, 81 per cent of respondents said they felt that most politicians didn't take into account the views of ordinary people. Among Leave voters, the figure was 91 per cent.[42]

Sometimes, blowback is inevitable.

So, where do we go from here? Well, the liberals and progressives may, if they so choose, persist in dismissing those who rocked the boat as racists, fascists, reactionaries and nativists. They may plough on determinedly while reassuring themselves of their own virtue in the face of the 'mob'. But until they grasp that the grievances that gave rise to the anger and resentment must ultimately be addressed, lest these things intensify, we will not see a rapprochement.

The resounding victory of Boris Johnson's Conservative Party at the 2019 general election came about in large part because they convinced working-class Britain that it was finally being heard. Brexit would be 'done', and democracy would prevail. It was a message that resonated loudly. But the bitterness and sense of disenfranchisement that developed over many years will not suddenly dissipate just through Brexit being enacted. There is a mountain of other complaints and injustices that must be tackled if working-class discontent is to be assuaged. Tory intimations of a future strategy designed to pitch towards working-class communities – with the obvious intention of embedding their support – are yet to be tested. Actions will speak louder than words.

All of this does, however, pose some deep and searching questions for the Left. The tasks confronting it now are to overcome the fragmentation caused by globalisation and to understand why there exists among the working class a hankering for something beyond individual rights and money; to build a common good and to speak again the language of One Nation; to recognise that most working-class people are social and parochial beings with a strong sense of place and cultural attachment, for whom relationships, work, family and community mean something very profound. The challenge then is to develop a programme around these realities.

The Left must return urgently to the politics of belonging. It needs to recognise why the working class roared. It needs also to open its ears to working-class anxieties and to understand what drives them, to stop dismissing legitimate concerns with cliché, abuse and contempt, to break the group-think that has infected its ranks and resulted in a toxic atmosphere that encourages constant displays of faux outrage while constraining free speech and honest debate around contentious issues (all themes that I shall explore in greater detail in the following pages).

If it does these things, the Left might begin to win back the hearts and minds of the millions of working-class people who have deserted it.

As a start, it would do well to examine what happened in a corner of east London in the early years of this century.

# 2

# We Need to Talk About Immigration

You wouldn't think it from strolling around the place today, but the town of Barking was once one of the world's largest fishing ports. During its nineteenth-century heyday, it was home to a fleet of around 200 vessels, which plied their trade from the banks of the Thames estuary and out into the North Sea. Fishing boats from Barking were known to travel as far afield as Iceland.

The names of pubs dotted around the town – most long since bulldozed – stood as a testament to its proud seafaring history: the Fisherman's Arms, the Short Blue, the Fishing Smack, the Barge Aground, the Lighterman, the Jolly Fisherman, the Blue Anchor. Captain James Cook had famously been married in 1762 in the parish church – St Margaret's – located in the grounds of a prominent seventh-century abbey, the ruins of which can still be visited today.

In the 1920s, London County Council – under pressure to rehouse families displaced by the slum clearances in the East End – purchased a vast area of farmland straddling Barking and its village neighbour a couple of miles to the east, Dagenham, on which it built 26,000 homes. The Becontree Estate had been born. It was eventually to become the largest municipal housing estate in the world.

With its endless uniform streets of solid, brick-built, modest but spacious terraced houses, the place became home to thousands of working-class families, many of whom – including both sets of my own grandparents and one set of great-grandparents – had travelled the short distance down the line from gritty East End districts such as Bow, Mile End and Stepney.

Many felt they had struck gold. Their new homes had indoor toilets and gardens front and back. Everything was pristine. As the estate expanded, there would be, every few blocks, a newly built library or pub, an immaculate little shopping parade or a public park. The Ford motor company opened its huge plant down by Dagenham Dock in 1931, and it soon became the area's foremost employer. If you didn't work at Ford, you knew someone who did. The borough of Barking (formally renamed Barking and Dagenham in 1980) was about as working class as it gets. Naturally, the place was a Labour heartland.

Though it could never be described as affluent, the borough was rich in other ways. The shared backgrounds and cultural familiarity fostered a deep sense of community and cohesion that is always a hallmark of those societies most at ease with themselves. Employment levels were decent, with plentiful jobs in local blue-collar industries, and there weren't the wide disparities in wealth that sometimes blighted other communities.

Neighbours knew each other. They talked on the street and over the garden fence. Local institutions – clubs, societies, churches – thrived. One such, the Dagenham Girl Pipers, achieved international recognition. Football was the most popular pastime for local boys, and the streets of Barking and Dagenham would spawn a host of footballing icons, including Alf Ramsey, Bobby Moore, Jimmy Greaves and Terry Venables.

The deep social and cultural homogeneity engendered a spirit of reciprocity and belonging among local citizens. There was a common – and often unspoken – understanding and affinity. You were part of something greater than yourself. If you did something that broke the moral code, it was likely to induce a sense of shame not only in yourself but for your family too. Relationships – within families and between them – mattered. When someone died, their loved ones would post a notice in the deceased's front garden, officially announcing the loss and thanking neighbours for their condolences and flowers.

The local council was a real presence, setting down strict rules for tenants and employing an army of workmen to ensure things stayed neat and tidy. Streets were unlittered, the privet hedges that bordered every front garden were regularly trimmed, and from time to time every council home would be redecorated. Annual prizes were awarded for the best-kept gardens. This was municipal socialism in action. Outsourcing was a term not yet invented.

None of this is to unduly romanticise the place. As with all working-class communities, Barking and Dagenham experienced its share of social problems and privations. But, above everything, it was a settled, stable community – and that stability owed much to the common bonds of background, custom, tradition, language and social mores that existed between its people.

It was into this settled and stable community that I was born in 1974. I grew up on the Becontree Estate, on Goresbrook Road, in the shadow of the Ford plant. Even now I can name the families who lived on our section of the street when I was a boy: on one side of us the Shirleys, Mrs Maddison, the Bests, the Palmers, Mrs Smith, Mrs Martin, Mrs Angliss, the Horrigans; and on the other Mrs Holdup, the Cuttings, the Johnsons, Nellie Anderson, the Taylors, the Ellises and the Reeces. Our family knew all of them, and we spoke to them whenever we saw them.

When I moved away from the borough in 2009, I knew only the neighbours immediately adjacent to me.

For the first 25 years of my life in Barking and Dagenham, the place was, in a cultural sense at least, unchanging. Though some other east London boroughs – such as neighbouring Newham and Redbridge and, further afield, Tower Hamlets and Hackney – had undergone a process of deep ethnic and cultural change since the Second World War, Barking and Dagenham still bore all the characteristics of those early days of the Becontree Estate. It remained overwhelmingly white working class and culturally homogeneous. At my primary school – Monteagle, with 400 pupils – I remember an Asian boy as the only student from a minority ethnic background. I relay these things merely as statements of fact.

My family's social network stretched well beyond our street. We were friendly with the families of school friends and teammates from the local football clubs for which my brother and I played. We would socialise with them regularly. Both sets of grandparents lived just the other side of Becontree underground station, and we would be constant visitors to their homes. We knew their neighbours too. As with many others who had moved to the estate in the 1930s, my grandparents had made the place their home and saw out the rest of their lives there.

Work, family and community were the fundamental pillars upon which people's lives were built. For those with limited wealth and opportunities, such things always take on so much more meaning. There was an underpinning sense of place and belonging felt by those living on the Becontree Estate. We were rooted. We were parochial. We were among family and friends. People looked out for each other, and there was a tangible social solidarity.

## A community fragments

But it wasn't to last. In the early part of this century, things began to change. For this period signalled the beginning of what became a very deep-seated shift in both the demographic and cultural life of the borough. It is a challenge to convey in prose the sheer rapidity and extent of the transformation that took place in Barking and Dagenham in the decade after 2000 and the impact it had on the local population.

This was a time when the effects of globalisation and a more liberal approach to immigration, embodied by EU freedom of movement laws, were beginning to be felt. And in Barking and Dagenham those effects were acute. Car production at the Ford plant was on its last legs, and what was once a stable, cohesive and enduring community was suddenly racked by social instability and fragmentation.

Streets and neighbourhoods changed beyond recognition and with breath-taking speed as thousands of newcomers arrived into the borough. Most of these new arrivals – from places such as Poland, Lithuania and Nigeria – were fundamentally decent, hardworking and law-abiding people; but beyond narrow economic status, they often they had little in common with those who had long lived in the community they had joined. They looked, spoke and lived their lives differently.

Barking and Dagenham's cultural homogeneity was starting to disintegrate. The steady constancy that had served the borough so well for so long was slowly shattering as it suddenly found itself in the eye of the storm of the national debate around globalisation and immigration.

I witnessed these events first-hand. At first, I was untroubled by what was happening around me. Why wouldn't I be? I was, after all, an enthusiastic twenty-something political activist on the Left. I welcomed the change. This was cosmopolitan liberalism in action. It was 'vibrant' and 'progressive'. Our strength lay in our new diversity, didn't it? Forward to the new world, in which the enlightened minority imposed overdue social and cultural change on the reactionary natives of Barking and Dagenham, and places like it, with their small 'c' conservative ways and sentimental ideas about place and belonging.

In argument, I would deploy all the usual slogans of the young, headstrong radical who is certain he is right. 'Migrants are not to blame!' . . . 'Don't pander to the racists!' . . . 'Workers have more in common with each other than with the bosses!' and so on.

I thought of these statements as clinchers in debates with my fellow citizens. No reasonable person would ever disagree with them, surely. And here's the point: no one ever did. That's because, in every sense possible, they missed the point.

No one blamed migrants, because they accepted that those migrants were not personally responsible for the situation. Indeed, local people often demon-strated a clear-eyed understanding of why a migrant family living in a poor country might wish to uproot themselves in an effort to seek a better life. 'I'd probably do it myself if I was in their position', was a common refrain.

No one was pandering to racists. Most local people opposed completely the idea that some of their fellow humans should be treated less favourably on account of the colour of their skin.

And no one denied that – in a strict economic sense, at least – workers of all backgrounds had more in common with each other than they did with their bosses. But this ignored the reality that most workers didn't see themselves merely as some kind of stage army in a war against capitalism. They were social and parochial beings for whom a sense of cultural attachment – around such things as tradition, custom, language and religion – meant much. In the end, economic factors are far from the only consideration when it comes to what may unite (or, indeed, divide) people.

That's why, whenever I trotted out these clichés in debate – and I did it to the point of tedium – people would often roll their eyes and turn away. I just wasn't getting it. When my friends and neighbours complained about the sudden upheaval in their community and the rupturing of social bonds, they were not blaming migrants, nor pandering to racism, nor taking the side of 'the bosses'. Rather, they were criticising the system that had brought this situation upon them. In particular, they were attacking politicians for turning a blind eye to their predicament.

The social and demographic convulsions led to a profound sense of bewilderment and disorientation in Barking and Dagenham. Inexcusably, liberal politicians and media commentators presented this reaction as being driven by innate racism and xenophobia. It was, for the most part, anything but. Local people felt the way they did because their sense of *order*, and not their sense of *race*, had been violated.

Week after week, the letters page of the local news-paper, the *Barking and Dagenham Post*, would be filled with the pleadings of residents seeking respite, beseeching politicians to pay heed to them and address their concerns. In response, they were told that there was no alternative: this was how the world worked these days, and it would be foolish to even attempt to intervene and change it. To add insult to injury, they were patronised with arguments about how globalisation of this kind would ultimately benefit them though improved GDP and cultural enrichment – as if these things were all that mattered.

The statistics underline the degree to which the place was transformed so quickly. Between 2001–11, the non-UK-born population of Barking and Dagenham increased by 205 per cent – the biggest percentage increase across London during that period, and almost double that of the borough which saw the second-highest increase (Greenwich at 103 per cent). During the same period, Barking and Dagenham experienced the highest percentage increase, at 169 per cent, of all London boroughs in the non-UK-born share of all residents,[1] again far ahead of the borough with the next highest increase (Havering at 83 per cent). The increase in the share had risen further to 230 per cent by 2017.[2]

In 2001, 80.86 per cent of all residents in the borough identified as 'White British'. Within just a decade, they had become a minority at 49.46 per cent. This decrease in the White British population was the largest for any local authority in England and Wales.[3] In the council ward in which I lived at the time – Thames – the figure for White British plunged from 74.9 per cent in 2001 to 37.1 per cent in 2011.[4] (It is important to say here that I am using the census classification of White British only so far as it provides the best available guide to the dramatic demographic shifts in Barking and Dagenham during this time, and the degree to which native citizens became marginalised. Beyond that, the question of skin colour should, of course, be considered irrelevant.)

Forecasts by the Office for National Statistics show that the total population in Barking and Dagenham will rise by 15.4 per cent in the years 2016–26 – the third highest percentage increase of all local authorities in England.[5] This means that the number of people in this already populous, hard-pressed working-class borough will have surged by 47 per cent from 163,944 to 240,300 between 2001 and 2026. By 2041, the White British population in Barking and Dagenham is projected to stand at just 23 per cent.[6] The 2021 census will, when it is published, surely reveal more startling statistics about Barking and Dagenham in the way of population shifts over the previous decade.

The sudden and substantial growth in the number of residents inevitably caused increased pressure on housing and local services. GP surgeries and schools particularly began to feel the strain. On one occasion, I was asked by a close relative to assist him in securing a nursery place for his daughter. He had lived in the borough all his life. But the local authority had informed him that, such was the pressure on places owing to recent surges in the population (including a rise of almost 50 per cent in the number of children aged four or under between 2001 and 2011[7]), all capacity was exhausted locally, and the only option was to place his child in a nursery outside the borough. My relative did not blame the new arrivals; but he did blame politicians who had allowed it to come to this.

I am certain that many across the borough experienced similar challenges. The profound belief among local folk in the principle of reciprocity meant that when it came to, for example, the allocation of social housing stock, it was not unreasonable to confer some kind of advantage on those who had been resident in the borough for longest. There was a widespread sentiment that the individuals and families who had lived in and sustained the borough over many years should be at the front of the queue over those who had just arrived. When local people witnessed their own sons and daughters struggling to get a foot on the housing ladder while some newcomers, because of their own circumstances, were given priority status, it bred resentment.

Those on the Left who at least recognised that such real-life problems existed, and didn't just dismiss them with glib arguments about economic and cultural enrichment, often responded with generalised statements about how capitalism was ultimately to blame and government should invest more in public services to accommodate the extra demand. To a degree they were right, of course. But employing this kind of boilerplate, ideological response did nothing to assuage the immediate concerns of most people who simply wanted swift relief from the acute effects of the population increase and didn't particularly want to wait for capitalism to be smashed before it came. Neither did these solely economic prescriptions address the very real social and cultural challenges that were being thrown up by such rapid and intense change.

### The far-right takes advantage

And so it was that at the local elections in 2006, thousands of voters in Barking and Dagenham – ignored, neglected and scorned – took what they felt was the only action left available to them. They voted for the British National Party (BNP), and did so in their thousands. Twelve BNP councillors were returned, including two in the ward – Goresbrook – in which I had grown up. Remarkably, the party had stood only thirteen candidates out of a possible fifty-one, yet it now formed the official opposition on Barking and Dagenham council – its best achievement in local government. Had it run a full slate of candidates, locals will tell you, there is every possibility it would have won control.

In the run-up to the elections, the BNP had presented itself as the only party willing to listen to, and act upon, the concerns of locals. It spoke the language of place, community, tradition, belonging and identity. Moreover, it wasn't afraid to speak out against mass immigration. As usual, the party did its best to hide its murky, thuggish past and be seen as a mainstream voice of common sense. And the more it was derided and attacked by the liberal establishment, the more it endeared itself to local voters.

The count for these elections took place in a school almost directly opposite my old family home. Images of jubilant BNP councillors were beamed directly into the homes of the nation and splashed across the pages of the next day's newspapers. A few years previous, such a spectacle would have been unthinkable in Barking and Dagenham. It seemed a bitter irony that the school was named after a former long-serving local Labour MP.

Until 2004, when it won a single seat in a council by-election, the BNP had never managed to get a foothold in the borough. Like the National Front, it had penetrated other boroughs in east London, but the far-right had always found the door to Barking and Dagenham firmly shut. Not so now. The place was fertile territory.

But in spite of these wake-up calls, little changed. Local politicians were, in any case, restricted in their capacity to respond to what were decisions and phenomena taking place at a national – sometimes international – level. But where national politicians had the scope to intervene, even in some small way, they refused to do so. 'No compromise with the racists of Barking and Dagenham', seemed to be the message.

Some politicians would occasionally trot out platitudes about how 'we must listen to people's concerns on immigration'. But what people wanted was *action* – some kind of remedial measures to alleviate the pressure and pace of change. This never came. The politicians had no answers beyond sticking to the script of lecturing people about the economic and cultural benefits of their new environment.

Locals saw the words of politicians for what they were: glib, patronising and dismissive. They realised that these politicians were merely paying lip service to them and, in reality, no one was going to come to their aid. So, resigned to their fate, thousands of residents simply upped sticks and left. In the decade 2001–11, there was a mass exodus of people from Barking and Dagenham, as over 40,000 residents departed.[8] These included members of my own family and many friends. Folk who had been rooted in the streets, workplaces and local institutions of the borough for generations had had enough. They left what, for many, had been the only home they had ever known, and headed for places such as Kent or the Essex coast (Clacton-on-Sea has since become known as 'Little Dagenham').

I often think that if such a phenomenon had occurred in affluent, middle-class Henley-on-Thames or Guildford or Harrogate, there would almost certainly have been some kind of inquiry. Questions would have been asked about what was persuading so many local residents to flee their home town. But this was Barking and Dagenham, where people were working class and attitudes 'reactionary'. So no one took any notice.

Undoubtedly not everyone who fled from the borough during these years did so because of the impact of immigration – some probably moved away after deciding to cash-in on their decision to purchase their council homes in the 1980s under Margaret Thatcher's Right-to-Buy scheme – but there can be no denying that immigration was the motivating factor in the choice of many. I know it, because they told me so.

The migration away from places such as Barking and Dagenham during this period was often depicted by the liberal media as 'white flight'. In fact, it was no such thing. Colour was irrelevant to most local people. When it came to relationships with fellow citizens, what mattered to them was something much greater than skin pigmentation – something rooted in social and cultural solidarity, a common understanding of place, tradition and custom, the shared values on which the most cohesive and stable societies are built. As things changed in Barking and Dagenham, many locals found that, as a consequence of language differences, they were simply unable to hold meaningful conversations with their new neighbours. When they left, it wasn't a flight from non-whiteness; rather, it was a flight to familiarity.

They left a borough which had become fractured and atomised – a place in which there were no riots or civil unrest, but where residents often now lived parallel lives, estranged from their neighbours.

Some older residents remained – generally those who lacked the money, energy or inclination to start life anew elsewhere. Women who had lived in the borough for sixty years or more, whose husbands had died and children had flown the nest, suddenly found themselves living lives of loneliness and isolation. An assortment of languages were now spoken along their streets; interactions with their fellow citizens, which for many had always been a central and reassuring feature of their daily lives, became much less frequent; local shops they had patronised for years had disappeared, to be replaced with outlets selling foreign foods or other things of which they had no need. My local pub – the Crooked Billet, a once-popular establishment steeped in history – eventually became an Eastern European restaurant. Most other pubs also closed their doors.

In this context, it isn't difficult to see why the message that local people heard from the political and cultural elites – that they should embrace this new 'vibrant' multiculturalism as an enriching ingredient of a diverse, modern Britain – failed to resonate with them. It wasn't that they objected to living alongside people who were different, or to experiencing alternative cultures; it was that they expected any change to take place in moderation and at a pace that didn't violate their own sense of belonging and stability. Instead of this, a whirlwind was allowed to whip through Barking and Dagenham over these few short years. And the real tragedy is that the failure of politicians to address – or even recognise – the concerns of locals unleashed a reaction that, in the end, gave succour and influence to the far-right. A community that would have comfortably absorbed a sensible and modest number of new arrivals and cultures instead became a happy hunting ground for real racists and fascists looking to exploit local anger and frustration.

In 2014, Barking played host to the BBC's political discussion programme *Question Time*.[9] A woman in the audience, Pam Dumbleton, asked: 'Isn't it time the government listened to the people about the impact immigration is having in changing our communities?' When pressed by the show's chairman, David Dimbleby, to elaborate, Ms Dumbleton added: 'The government haven't got a clue. David Cameron has never been to Barking ... The government need to come and walk through our town and just see how we now live. Go back twelve years; it was totally different.' During the panel's responses, another audience member, a middle-aged local man, intervened: 'Listen to the indigenous people here, the people that have been here all their lives', he pleaded. He went on to criticise what he perceived as the disproportionate government assistance afforded to newcomers, at which point he was noisily rebuked. Desperate still to make his case, the audience member explained that he was homeless and saw it as unfair that, as a local man, he was being neglected by the government in favour of others. He had applied unsuccessfully for a hundred jobs, he said. The man's language was sharp; his tone belligerent. He was angry. When the panellist and *Times* columnist David Aaronovitch – a loyal foot soldier of the liberal elite army, if ever there was one – upbraided him for 'blaming the wrong people', the man responded that he wasn't blaming immigrants at all and was not a racist. His contempt was plainly aimed at the government rather than individual immigrants. Anyone willing to give him a fair hearing could see precisely the point he was trying – albeit imperfectly – to make. 'Why is a street not yours because some of the faces in it are black?' Aaronovitch hit back, illustrating that he had completely missed the point. The audience member had never mentioned black faces.

Seconds later, the man gave up. He donned his coat and walked off the set. It was an example in micro-cosm of how the people of places such as Barking and Dagenham had been patronised by the liberal and cultural elites to the point of exasperation. Voice concerns about the massive changes to your community, and be branded a racist who dislikes black people.

The utter failure of the political class to deal with the concerns of residents such as Pam Dumbleton and her fellow audience member meant that the entire debate around immigration became toxic in places such as Barking and Dagenham. Grievances were left to fester, resentment to breed.

As it turned out, the BNP hung around for just a few years in the borough before disappearing. The party's fate was sealed by a combination of its own spectacular implosion at a national level, the decampment of many locals who had voted for it at the 2006 elections and – perhaps to a lesser degree – Labour Party activists and anti-racist organisations targeting the area with concerted leafleting and door-knocking campaigns. Labour soon reasserted its hegemony across Barking and Dagenham. But it was now a very different borough – virtually unrecognisable from that which had existed around the end of the 1990s. Older traditional Labour voters had become considerably fewer, supplanted by their younger, more liberal and cosmopolitan counterparts.

Even so, much of the resentment remained. As I noted in Chapter 1, Leave won 62 per cent of the vote in Barking and Dagenham at the EU referendum in 2016. Anyone with the slightest understanding of the place and its recent history could have seen this coming a mile off. (It is important to note here, too, that Barking and Dagenham was not an outlier in this respect. Other parts of the UK which had experienced similarly high levels of immigration in recent years also recorded some of the biggest Leave votes – for example, the local authority areas covering the towns of Boston in Lincolnshire and

Wisbech in Cambridgeshire voted 76 per cent and 69 per cent respectively in favour of Leave.)

I still return to Barking and Dagenham from time to time. On one such occasion, a few years back, I was approached by a man as I was walking towards the Tesco supermarket on Highbridge Road (I seem to recall he wanted the time, or a light for his cigarette, or something). Before making his request, he asked, 'Excuse me, do you speak English?' It was something of a jaw-dropping moment. Just a decade or so previous, such a question as a conversation-opener in Barking and Dagenham would have been inconceivable.

On another occasion, more recently, I took my own children back to the area. We spent a couple of hours in a local park near Barking town centre. Our visit was notable for the fact that, in the hours we spent there, and in the many voices and conversations we heard, nobody spoke in English. *Literally* nobody. It reaffirmed to me the dramatic extent to which the area had changed, and so quickly. I tried to put myself in the shoes of an elderly long-term resident of the borough and imagine how this radical transformation might have felt for him or her.

The borough has hit the headlines over recent years for being the home of a notorious gang of criminal Albanian drug traffickers – 'Hellbanianz' – and also of one of the terrorists behind the London Bridge attacks in 2017.

Pages have been set up on Facebook on which former locals, now scattered to the four winds, reminisce about their days in the borough. Many of the conversations take a similar theme: proud to have come from there, knew all of our neighbours, moved away when the area changed, all my friends left too, went back there recently, not the place I knew, and so on. No doubt former residents of towns and villages throughout Britain engage in the same kind of nostalgic musings, but there is no question that the sense of loss among one-time citizens of Barking and Dagenham is more profound than for most.

Our political class failed the people of Barking and Dagenham, and places like it, badly. Such communities are still brimming with anger and bitterness. We see it in our nation's current polarisation. The crucial challenge confronting us, then – and one that, even today, too many politicians appear too scared to tackle – is how to foster the kind of spirit of community and shared values in these places that, on the one hand, welcomes new arrivals and opposes racism and prejudice steadfastly, while, on the other, recognising the justified resistance of long-term residents to the type of sudden social and cultural change that has the capacity to violently disrupt their sense of place, order and belonging.

The first step is to begin a brutally honest conversation about the impact of mass immigration on working-class communities such as that of Barking and Dagenham – one that isn't dominated by cliché and recrimination. But such is the degree of group-think and dogmatism among many on the modern Left, the signs are not hopeful that they would be willing to engage in such a dialogue. Their approach to this topic is too often one of name-calling and smear rather than a hard-headed examination of the facts.

### Pressure on wages: time for an honest discussion

Such a conversation, should it ever occur, must not be allowed to dismiss inconvenient truths, nor seek to suffocate the views of opponents. It must instead be rooted in evidence and reason.

For a start, it must dispense with false rhetoric which seeks to claim that there can be no economic downsides to mass immigration. In reality, the issues around this are complex. Such evidence that exists suggests that, overall, the link between immigration and wages is broadly negligible, but this conclusion can often disguise the reality that the effects on certain – and often the poorer – sections of the native population are more appreciable.

For example, a study conducted by the Bank of England in 2015 concluded that for every 10 percentage point rise in the proportion of immigrants working in semi-skilled or unskilled jobs, there is a 2 per cent reduction in pay.[10] This reduction may seem trifling to some, but for those already earning low wages, it can represent an appreciable financial blow. An earlier study by a team of academics at the London School of Economics concluded that migrant workers already in the UK were themselves most likely to suffer any adverse wage effects arising from immigration.[11]

After the Leave vote in 2016, evidence emerged, including in the form of a study by the Chartered Institute of Personnel and Development,[12] showing that a slowdown in the rate of EU workers coming to the UK had contributed to a tighter labour market, which in turn had forced many employers to increase wages. There can be little doubt that this slowdown was responsible for some of the sharpest increases in salaries in certain sectors – such as catering and hospitality and construction – in which high numbers of migrant workers were employed.[13] In 2018, a review of previous studies by the government's Migration Advisory Committee showed that while the impact of immigration on average wages was small, the effect on wage *distribution* was more significant, with low-paid workers losing out and higher-paid workers gaining.[14]

Taken together, all of this represented a body of evidence demonstrating that the EU's free movement laws and wider immigration policy had negatively affected the wage packets of at least some British workers, and in some cases to a potentially significant degree. Yet those figures throughout the labour movement – including many trade union leaders – who had long rejected any suggestion that higher levels of immigration might carry economic downsides for some workers remained silent. There was no acknowledgement, as these facts began to materialise, that they might have got it wrong. Instead, they stuck to trotting out the usual disingenuous injunctions imploring people not to 'blame migrants'. But to argue that mass immigration had depressed wages, which it had, was not to blame migrants personally for that outcome – any more than to argue that unemployment holds down wages, which it does, is to blame the unemployed. It is to make a simple statement of fact.

The moral bankruptcy of trade union leaders on this subject borders on the criminal. Their role in life is to secure for their members the most favourable wages and conditions. But where that objective conflicted with their own personal ideology – in this case their support for open borders – they put the ideology first. For many of them, maintaining the purity of their own worldview was given primacy over the interests of their members.

They aren't alone in their wilful myopia. Today's Left is, sadly, full of worthy activists who demonstrate a stubborn unwillingness to face facts on this issue. So they will insist, for example, that low wages are caused only by 'rip-off bosses' and that better regulation – such as a higher minimum wage – and trade union organisation are the way to address the problem. Of course trade unionists and socialists should always campaign for improved workplace regulation and higher levels of trade union membership. But that takes us only so far. Ultimately, employers will always be under less pressure to pay higher wages the greater the supply of labour available to them. Better regulation and trade union organisation does not change that simple reality. As the Irish Congress of Trade Unions was honest enough to admit in a submission to the Irish government over proposed labour market reforms: 'It is an iron law of economics that an abundant supply of labour pushes down its cost. It is insulting people's intelligence to pretend otherwise.'[15]

Increasing the minimum wage – welcome though it would be – does not provide a complete solution to these problems. Most workers already earn above the minimum wage, yet many still experience downward pressure on their wages as a consequence of an over-supply of labour. So how would these workers stand to gain from an increase?

Former US presidential candidate Bernie Sanders – a hero to many on the Left – has also recognised the truth that a policy of open borders drives down wages, telling an interviewer in 2015 that it was 'a Koch brothers' proposal. That's a right-wing proposal that says, essentially, "There is no United States."' When the interviewer ventured that such a policy would make the global poor richer, Sanders retorted:

> And it would make everybody in America poorer. You're doing away with the concept of the nation state ... What right-wing people in this country would love is an open border policy, bringing in all kinds of people working for two or three dollars an hour. That would be great for them.[16]

Often, defenders of mass immigration will invoke the argument known as the 'lump of labour fallacy'. This argument recognises – correctly – that there isn't a fixed number of jobs in an economy, and that we should therefore be wary of crude arguments suggesting that 'migrants are stealing our jobs'. But the theory then goes that increases in the population, such as through immigration, will inevitably lead to more demand throughout the economy, which in turns leads to more jobs and higher levels of growth and prosperity. Aside from it being an argument for an ever-expanding population, this part of the theory has been effectively debunked, notably by the Cambridge economist Robert Rowthorn, who, in his 2015 book *The Costs and Benefits of Large-Scale Immigration*, explained how a study of the data showed that:

> the extra jobs may not appear immediately and there may be quite a long transition period during which native workers experience unemployment (or lower wages). Moreover, if there is a continuing inflow of migrants, the labour market may be in constant disequilibrium, with economic growth and new job creation lagging constantly behind the growth in labour supply due to immigration. In its extreme form the 'lump of labour fallacy' may well be a fallacy, but it points to a genuine issue.[17]

And in response to the common argument that the UK needs a relaxed immigration policy to guarantee an inflow of workers who will generate the taxes and provide the labour necessary to sustain a growing and aging population, Rowthorn points out what ought really to be obvious:

> young immigrants who enter the UK during the initial years eventually reach old age and new immigrants are then required simply to preserve the age structure. Rejuvenation through immigration is an endless

treadmill. To maintain a once and for all reduction in the dependency ratio requires a never ending stream of immigrants. Once the inflow stops, the age structure will revert to its original trajectory.[18]

By enabling the unrestricted transfer of workers from low- to high-wage economies, free movement of labour across the EU has proved to be a bosses' dream, allowing them to hold down wages to the detriment of native workers. It is no coincidence that the flows of labour are much greater from low-wage eastern Europe to higher-wage western Europe than they are the other way round. It is like a system of outsourcing in reverse: no longer are companies forced to relocate abroad in order to benefit from cheaper labour costs; free movement gives them the ability to achieve it while staying put.

In an interview with BBC Radio 5 Live's *Wake Up to Money* in February 2019, a former UK managing director of supermarket chain Lidl, Ronny Gottschlich, was quite candid about the opportunities that free movement provided in the way of reducing labour costs, telling the programme:

> The grocery/retail sector in large parts of Britain is dependent on a foreign workforce, and if this workforce isn't there anymore ... your cheap labour falls away ... and this would ultimately lead to higher wages ... There's no doubt if you wouldn't have had the labour available from other parts of the European Union, this would have ultimately had to lead to a higher wage because you would need to attract employees from, let's say, Britain to work in your stores.

Free movement of labour is – alongside free movement of goods, capital and services – one of the four indivisible 'freedoms' enshrined in EU Single Market rules. Such an arrangement ultimately places workers in the same category as copper and coffee – commodities to be traded in the interests of the powerful and wealthy.

And the downsides of free movement are experienced not only by the richer economies, but by poorer ones too. Eastern European countries have, in some cases, suffered depopulation crises, with crippling labour shortages affecting their smooth functioning and prosperity. For example, a report in the *Guardian* in April 2019 highlighted the crisis inflicted on Romania's health service as a consequence of the emigration of 43,000 doctors since the country's accession to the EU.[19] And Latvia lost around a fifth of its population in the years after EU accession.[20]

In the end, a system of free movement of labour between highly diverse economies leads inexorably to large numbers of workers migrating from the lower-wage economies to the higher-wage economies, with the resultant problems for both types of economy. It is not racist to point out this simple truth.

## *Going backwards on productivity*

An abundance of cheap labour also has the effect of stunting productivity growth. As a 2017 report by the Institute for Public Policy Research put it: 'it has become too easy and too cheap to raise output by adding a low-wage worker rather than by investing in new technology or innovating in workplace organisation'.[21] This can be seen, for example, with the proliferation of hand car washes, often staffed by Eastern Europeans paid little more than a pittance. Though himself a supporter of free movement, the left-wing journalist and activist Paul Mason has highlighted how, in this particular example, low wages have discouraged investment and technological advance. As Mason argues:

> A car wash used to mean a machine. Now it means five guys with rags. There are now 20,000 hand car washes in Britain, only a thousand of them regulated. By contrast, in the space of 10 years, the number of rollover car-wash machines has halved – from 9,000 to 4,200. The free-market economic model, combined with a globalised labour market, has produced a kind of reverse industrialisation.[22]

Likewise with the fruit-picking industry. Champions of free movement (and of the EU generally) were at pains to warn us in the wake of the referendum that fruit would be left to rot in fields if the plentiful supply of labour from Europe was shut off. British workers just wouldn't be willing to do such menial work, they argued. What they meant was that British workers were probably unwilling to do the work for the pittance that was on offer, but saying so explicitly would have contradicted their argument that free movement doesn't depress wages.

In 2018, the BBC reported how, as a consequence of several countries having experienced a shortage of agricultural labour, investment was being made in developing robots which could pick fruit just as quickly and efficiently as humans. It was another example of how cheap labour had led to 'reverse industrialisation'. Now, suddenly deprived of that labour, producers were forced to either pay higher wages or invest in new technology.[23]

The degree to which the Left has so rapidly and dramatically shifted its position on the question of open borders is remarkable. It wasn't so long ago that support for regulation of the labour supply was mainstream across the Left. Many socialists and trade unionists understood that the labour supply was a market dynamic which, as with all market dynamics, needed to be regulated so as to secure the best outcome for workers. Regulation was also essential as a means to ensuring effective government planning around such things as housing, welfare, employment and so on. Any government that could not control or even accurately predict the numbers coming into the country was plainly at a disadvantage in this regard.

Support for open borders was traditionally a fringe position, espoused mainly by Trotskyists, anarchists and ultra-liberals. But now the reverse is true: a commitment to open borders is the default position on the Left, and regulation regarded as a shibboleth. Worse, those on the Left who still argue for regulation are frequently dismissed as 'nationalists' or 'nativists'.

The debate over EU free movement is a striking example of how many among the liberal and cultural elites assume that what may be beneficial for them must axiomatically be beneficial for everyone else. Thus, during the debate around Brexit, they would often make arguments such as: 'Why would we want to take away our own right to live and work in twenty-seven other countries? We must be mad.'

If you were one of the relatively small number of UK citizens who ever took advantage of this right, you might well ask that question. Often, these citizens had come from a more fortunate station in life – perhaps university-educated, of a middle-class background, working in a professional occupation, living in a more affluent part of the UK, unlikely to have ever experienced serious downward pressure on their wages through an over-supply of labour. But for many of the less privileged in society, free movement represented something very different: usually rapid and far-reaching change to their communities, with pressure on housing, local services and wages, for little in return. These citizens, not unreasonably, were willing to trade their automatic right to live and work in twenty-seven EU member states – a right that few of them, in any case, ever exercised – in return for control over immigration at home. Is that really so 'mad'?

Cheerleaders for EU free movement will often conveniently turn a blind eye to the fact that the EU itself is something of a fortress: stories of would-be migrants from outside the EU taking the most extraordinary risks, often at the cost of their own lives, in a desperate bid to enter EU territory are all too common. Indeed, one of the fascinating things about debating supporters of free movement is just how easy it is to expose the glaring inconsistencies at the heart of their argument. Ask them, for example, whether or not, if free movement is such a good thing, they would be happy for their government to extend it to every other nation on earth – thereby granting the right to live and work in the UK to billions – and watch them wriggle. Usually they will say 'No', and then defend that position by deploying the very same arguments – such as the inability of the country to cope with such numbers – that they deride opponents of EU free movement for making.

Similarly, ask them if they believe in the concept of the nation state at all and, if so, how a nation can even be a nation if it doesn't maintain borders; or whether or not there should be *any* limit on the numbers coming into the country (and, if so, what should it be, and how would it be enforced), and they will get themselves into all sorts of contradictory tangles.

An argument repeatedly trotted out by the defenders of open borders is that 'Britain has always been a nation of immigrants'. In making this assertion, proponents will cite the arrival and settlement of various groups over the centuries: Romans, Angles, Saxons, Vikings, Jutes, Normans, Jews, Irish, Huguenots, the Windrush generation, and so on. Of course, human history is such that all nations are nations of immigrants to a greater or lesser extent; but, in the case of Britain, this argument is often – and probably calculatedly – misleading. First, it glosses over the fact that the arrival of some of the aforementioned groups often created its own turmoil and tensions within the country. Second – and most pertinently – it ignores the dramatic disparities in the scale and pace of immigration throughout the ages, and particularly the fact that the level and intensity of immigration into Britain over the past twenty or so years is of an utterly different magnitude to that which was experienced before then. Even the numbers arriving during the period of post-war immigration from the Commonwealth were generally nothing like those of the period from the late 1990s onwards.

Figures published by the Office for National Statistics show that for the years between 1964 (when annual figures began to be collated) and 1997, net migration into the UK never rose above the tens of thousands, and often emigration would outstrip immigration. However, for the years 1998 to 2017, net migration figures were consistently in the hundreds of thousands – reaching a high of 332,000 in 2015.[24] For the last four of these years, the figures averaged 295,000 – the equivalent of a city the size of Newcastle. In the decade 2001–11 alone, the foreign-born population in the UK increased by just under 3 million – from 9 per cent to 13 per cent of the population.[25]

Migrants will generally settle in poorer, working-class areas, meaning that those areas suffer disproportionately from the increased strain on housing and public services. It is therefore no surprise that, as the numbers and intensity increased, so the demands from these communities – often the hard-pressed, post-industrial parts of the UK – for proper control grew louder.

As a consequence of the lack of control over immigration, faith in the system has collapsed. And the spectacle of politicians, when confronted over the issue, throwing their arms in the air and refusing to make a specific pledge on future numbers on the grounds that 'We shouldn't make promises that we cannot keep', means that the principle of democracy is undermined too. After all, what good are elected representatives if they cannot commit to doing something as fundamental as managing the nation's borders so as to control who is able to enter our territory?

### The myth of a prejudiced Britain

Increasingly in the UK, the debate around immigration is presented as being between two factions: one that is open, liberal and tolerant; the other closed, reactionary and prejudiced. But, in reality, things are nowhere near so simplistic. Evidence shows that most people in Britain are supportive of some form of immigration – but merely want it controlled to the degree that it doesn't cause sudden or profound social or economic disruption.

For example, a YouGov poll conducted in 2018 showed a complex picture, with 24 per cent agreeing that levels of immigration over the previous decade had been 'mostly good' for the UK, 32 per cent 'mostly bad', and the largest group – at 35 per cent – believing it had been 'both good and bad'. However, when asked their opinion on whether or not the level of immigration during that decade had been too high or too low, a clearer divide emerged, with 63 per cent agreeing it had been too high, 22 per cent believing it had been 'about right', and only 4 per cent holding the view that it had been too low.

The truth is that most Britons remain tolerant and welcoming. An ICM poll conducted immediately after the EU referendum – when you might have expected any prejudice, had it existed, to be at its most rampant – showed that 84 per cent of respondents, including, notably, 77 per cent of Leave voters, believed that EU nationals already living in Britain ought to be allowed to stay after the UK left the EU.[26] This points to a Britain whose people, far from being hostile and exclusionary, are imbued with a fundamental decency and fairness. They just feel that their good faith has been abused over many years by tin-eared politicians. These people are demonised for being 'anti-immigration' when most patently aren't. It is a sign of how a serious and analytical debate around this subject has become almost impossible. Emotion and hyperbole have taken the place of cool reasoning. When someone says, 'We should control our borders' or 'I support proper control of immigration', opponents will choose to interpret it as 'I oppose all immigration', or 'I don't like foreigners.'

Straw man arguments will be deployed in an effort to paint supporters of managed immigration as bigoted and unenlightened. For instance, after England won the cricket World Cup in 2019, several liberal commentators and celebrities took to Twitter to point out, patronisingly, that a number of the team's players were migrants. The message was clear: we wouldn't have won the World Cup but for immigration. If such arguments were aimed at only those in our society – a relatively tiny number – who were opposed to immigration in its entirety, they might be justified. But, as ever, they were targeted towards anyone who didn't favour completely open borders or who had raised concerns over the impact of *mass* immigration. The intention, of course, was to paint opponents of open borders and mass immigration as backward and narrow-minded.

The portrayal by some following the EU referendum of Britain as a cesspit of racism and xenophobia was always a grotesque caricature. In fact, many countries – including some in the EU itself – could learn a thing or two from Britain when it comes to levels of tolerance and opposition to prejudice. A study conducted by US researchers in 2019 found that hostility to immigrants was low in the UK, with 85 per cent of respondents saying they would be happy to have a foreign worker as a neighbour and 95 per cent someone from a different religion. This demonstrates the huge social progress that has been achieved in recent years and belies the depiction of a Britain steeped in 'hatred'. Co-author of the study Dr Jonathan Kelley said, 'There are many ways in which Britain is known to be "exceptional" in the European context, but prejudice against immigrants is clearly not one of them.'[27]

It is also worth noting that the UK was always pretty effective at increasing the ethnic diversity of the European Parliament, electing several candidates from black and minority ethnic backgrounds to serve in the place, in contrast to many EU countries which often sent none there.

The inherent fairness of the British people was also seen in their reaction to the 2018 Windrush scandal. The wrongful detention or deportation on Home Office instructions of a number of citizens generated an outpouring of sympathy, with 63 per cent even going so far as to say they were 'ashamed' of how Britain had treated the migrant victims.[28]

This chimed with a study by the Centre for Social Justice and Legatum Institute carried out in October 2016, which found that concerns over uncontrolled immigration were less about the migrants themselves than about the impact on wages, housing and public services. As one respondent told the study:

> I have seen, where I live, such a strain on public services. For example, schools, hospitals, doctors' surgeries, getting access to a GP and housing . . . It's nothing to do with where people come from. At some point you have to say enough is enough . . . We can't go on supporting people, several hundred thousand people, who choose to come here every year.[29]

And neither, as some would have us believe, are worries over the scale of immigration the preserve only of non-migrants. In 2013, the British Social Attitudes Survey found that 60 per cent of first- and second-generation migrants believed that immigration numbers should be reduced, with only 8 per cent believing they should be increased.[30]

This shows that migrants and their families are often entirely in step with the opinions of the wider native population over this issue. And why wouldn't they be? Why should we assume that those who happened to have settled in a new country themselves – not always through their own choice – would, as a result, desire a world of constant churn and rapid demographic change over the stability and order for which most people yearn? Enthusiasts for open borders should not be allowed to get away with implying they speak for all migrants in this debate. They do not.

In the eyes of many of our liberal politicians and commentators, it seems that a nation cannot be considered civilised if it exercises strict control over its borders or in any way encourages a national culture and recognises the desire of its citizens to feel part of it. By extension, it is assumed that any perception felt by those citizens that their culture might in some way be under threat can only originate from an innate xenophobia or racism.

But you need only look at a country such as Japan to see that this isn't the case. A highly civilised, advanced democracy, Japan maintains rigid control over immigration – not by closing its borders completely, but simply by ensuring the numbers are modest and manageable – while fostering a deep and abiding sense of patriotism and belonging among its people. A common and enduring culture, built on socially conservative values, helps to sustain a universal moral code. Japan is a nation whose citizens feel they are part of something greater than themselves. That belief, that sense of themselves as one nation and one people, transcends cold economic calculus (though it is also worth pointing out that much of Japan's post-war economic success was built around the type of Keynesian interventionism that any party of the mainstream Left could embrace). Ask the people of Japan whether they would wish to see their country become suddenly more liberal and cosmopolitan, and its borders more porous, and most would likely say no.

The Japanese do not obsess about the promotion of multiculturalism or diversity, yet immigrants and foreign visitors are generally well treated. The country is clean and safe. Crime rates and illegal drug use are low; wrongdoers are punished; and a breach of the moral code is likely to induce a sense of shame in the offender and his family.

Japan has its share of social problems of course – which country doesn't? – and good reason not to be proud of certain parts of its own history, but nobody would seriously argue that today's Japan is uncivilised or backward. On the contrary, it is one of the most unified and ordered nations on the planet – a testament to the idea that the nurturing of universal shared values and a sense of patriotism and belonging among a people does not automatically turn them into hostile and hate-filled nationalists.

During periods of economic downturn, Japan has never – unlike many other advanced nations – been seduced by the argument that in order to keep an economy thriving, head off population decline and support an aging population, a country must be willing to throw open its doors and invite large-scale immigration. The Japanese do not, it would appear, wish to see their country turned into a place that no longer resembles Japan. It is hard to sustain an argument that it is any the worse for that.

As I pointed out in Chapter 1, the champions of open borders and liberal cosmopolitanism will often assert that, in being responsible for generating improved levels of economic growth, their philosophy brings benefits to the entire nation, including the poorest. In other words, the working class ought really to be grateful to the elites for having forced this way of life on them. But, leaving aside the questionability of their claims over greater prosperity, this is to see the world through an extraordinarily narrow lens. It is to assume that working-class people elevate a desire for increased personal wealth above all else – above home, community, stability, tradition. Such a view betrays a striking ignorance of the values and priorities of the working class. Yes, of course they would be happy – wouldn't we all? – to see their wealth increase. But they do not seek this outcome at all costs – and certainly not at the expense of the things they hold dear. Man does not live by bread alone.

I once heard a fellow panellist at a debate venture that well-heeled liberals often see their nation as a shop whose main purpose is the transaction of business and whose inhabitants are mere customers, whereas working-class people are more inclined to see the nation as a home and their fellow citizens as family or housemates. This distinction in the priorities of the two groups, between the transactional and the relational, goes a long way to explaining why the debates around issues such as the EU and immigration have become so divisive.

The late senator Bobby Kennedy had it right when, rejecting the idea that economic considerations should trump all others, he told students at the University of Kansas in 1968:

> the gross national product does not allow for the health of our children, the quality of their education or the joy of their play. It does not include the beauty of our poetry or the strength of our marriages, the intelligence of our public debate or the integrity of our public officials. It measures neither our wit nor our courage, neither our wisdom nor our learning, neither our compassion nor our devotion to our country. It measures everything, in short, except that which makes life worthwhile. And it can tell us everything about America except why we are proud that we are Americans. If this is true here at home, so it is true elsewhere in [the] world.[31]

### It's not just the economy, stupid

It is also a grave error to assume – as many on today's Left seem to do – that an aversion to large-scale immigration is in truth the consequence of adverse economic conditions – such as those created by the global financial crisis – and nothing else. This argument goes that working-class concerns over immigration would evaporate if only we ended austerity or improved wages and invested enough so that the strain on housing and public services was eased.

But this is belied by the fact that these concerns have been expressed by the working class during times of growth and relative prosperity, and not only when the economy is in recession. For example, the election of twelve BNP councillors in Barking and Dagenham happened two years before the global crash and after more than a decade of consistent economic growth. Thus, responding to such concerns with trite rhetoric and slogans about how it's really all 'down to austerity' does little to assuage them.

Moreover, if it really was 'all about the economy', then Labour would have romped home in the 2017 and 2019 general elections, when its economic programme was more radical and redistributive than anything we have seen from a mainstream party in recent times. Instead, as I noted in Chapter 1, Labour has actually lost ground to the Tories in many of our less affluent constituencies. Concerns over high levels of immigration should not, therefore, be dismissed as though they were merely a proxy for other grievances.

In 2009, the former New Labour apparatchik Andrew Neather, a speech writer for Tony Blair, suggested that the sharp increase in immigration that occurred after the party won power in 1997 was a deliberate, but unspoken, policy. In an article published in the London *Evening Standard*, he wrote: 'It didn't just happen: the deliberate policy of ministers from late 2000 . . . was to open up the UK to mass migration.' Neather took part in discussions over a shift in immigration policy with other figures inside Labour's inner circle. He went on: 'I remember coming away from some discussions with the clear sense that the policy was intended – even if this wasn't its main purpose – to rub the Right's nose in diversity and render their arguments out of date.' For the Blair government, the liberalisation of immigration had the desired effect of creating a boom in the number of arrivals. 'But ministers wouldn't talk about it', continued Neather. 'In part, they probably realised the conservatism of their core voters: while ministers might have been passionately in favour of a more diverse society, it wasn't necessarily a debate they wanted to have in working men's clubs in Sheffield or Sunderland.'[32]

Twenty years later, the consequences of this controversial policy shift are all too evident. With the advent of immigration on a scale never before seen, a kaleidoscope was shaken violently in our country. The pieces still haven't fully settled – but one thing is sure: they aren't going to settle where the supporters of the policy expected them to.

In the end, those who wield power and influence in our society, and whose lives are often far removed from those whom their decisions impact most, must learn that imposing rapid and fundamental social and cultural change in working-class communities runs a high risk of violating the sense of place, order and belonging which has sustained those communities for generations and which still matters to many who live in them. So far there is little evidence that this reality has been understood.

For too long, the debate around immigration has been painted in primary colours, when in reality there are many shades of grey and much room for nuance. And even after the sustained public backlash against their open borders philosophy, so many on today's Left still fail to grasp the simple truth that rapid and large-scale movements of labour can, just like those of capital, cause deep social and economic disruption in working-class communities.

Relatively few in Britain wish to see all immigration stopped. And that is, of course, a good thing. But millions are crying out for a more patriotic, rooted, communitarian politics. They want to live in a nation in which common bonds exist between citizens; where family, relationships and social solidarity are elevated above narrow economic considerations; where shared values are promoted, tradition, stability and custom are respected, and newcomers are welcomed but encouraged to assimilate rather than stand apart. A nation that sees itself as a home, not a shop.

One Nation.

# 3

# A New National Religion: Liberal Wokedom

It was, I felt, a fairly straightforward point, even if I knew that many of my colleagues in the labour movement would disagree with it. The Labour Party had decided in a House of Commons vote to support a proposed Brexit deal with the EU which included the continuation of free movement. I tweeted my dismay:

> Labour comes out in favour of keeping free movement – an utter betrayal of traditional working-class people, the majority of whom oppose it and voted to end it in the referendum. The party will pay a heavy, but deserved, price for this at the ballot box.

No sooner had I posted the tweet than the keyboard warriors of the woke Left got to work. Straight out of the blocks was the journalist and activist Ash Sarkar, a self-professed 'literal communist', who replied: '"Traditional working-class"? jesus fucking christ paul, just say "white" with ya whole chest.'

Her intervention prompted a sustained outpouring of bile from others among the virtue-signalling ranks of Twitter, all certain that I really meant 'white' when I used the term 'traditional working class' and was simply couching my wicked racism in a euphemism. 'Buy yourself a brown shirt Paul, because there's a nationalist stain on your red one', wrote one prominent anti-Brexit activist. 'Simple equation here. If anyone opposes free movement it's because they're a racist', declared an author and playwright of modest renown.

It plainly didn't occur to these critics that in deciding that nobody who did not have white skin could ever be considered part of Britain's traditional working-class – not even those who had lived most or all of their lives here – they were laying bare their own prejudices. The fact, too, that, as I have shown elsewhere, a significant percentage of black and minority ethnic citizens themselves opposed open borders seemed lost on them. Their minds were made up: 'traditional working class' could only mean white folk, opponents of free movement were racist, and I was worthy of a Twitterstorm.

I had a similar experience a few months later at the Labour Party's annual conference in Brighton. While waiting to do an interview at the Sky News live point in the conference centre, I got talking to a thirty-something woman alongside me. 'Oh, you're that guy!' she said, after I introduced myself. 'The one who keeps going on about working-class values.' We attempted an exchange of views during which I tried to explain why working-class voters in our party's traditional heartlands – such as those I had grown up with in Barking and Dagenham – felt so alienated. But she didn't seem impressed. 'If you mean white people, you should just say white people', she grumbled, before we parted company. She was, by the way, a Member of Parliament.

On one level, these kinds of incidents are interesting, for they expose the degree of hysteria and intolerance that can be induced when people who are utterly certain that they are right are confronted with an unwelcome opinion. At the same time, however, they are illustrative of a much deeper sickness that now infects the modern Left from head to foot. It is the product of an unwavering belief among many of its activists in their own moral rightness, the certainty that their own views are so correct that they ought to be considered received wisdom – and, where necessary, enforced through legislation – and that alternative standpoints are inherently wrong and those who express them worthy of opprobrium.

It is no coincidence that this mindset has become prevalent across the Left at the same time as its institutions have become more and more dominated by the ranks of the liberal and progressive middle classes – with all that that entails in the way of outlook and priorities – and hollowed out of working-class representation.

This has meant, in turn, that traditional class-based politics has largely been dislodged by identity politics, as the Left has hurled itself into the battlegrounds of race, religion, sexuality, gender identity, 'hate speech', and the like. In doing so, it has taken much of the liberal establishment with it, so that our political discourse and public life are now increasingly mired in divisive squabbles and recriminations around these things. By extension, we see the fundamental right to freedom of expression coming under attack as never before, as a rigid conformity of opinion is demanded across the public sphere.

Ultimately, all of these things are connected, and the woke and institutional Left (which are increasingly the same thing) must take the lion's share of responsibility for the predicament in which we now find ourselves.

### The dead end of identity politics

Increasingly these days, society seeks to divide human beings into distinct identity groups and to view them exclusively through that prism when it comes to matters of political philosophy or their place in wider society. Much of our governing class is in the grip of this ideology. The political Right, for all its posturing and pretence at being 'anti-PC', has not only succumbed to it – the Right has its own influential liberal progressives, of course – but is in part responsible for its spread. Certainly the upsurge in identity politics has occurred under recent governments of all political hues and without any noticeable attempts by any of them to check it. That's because, in a nutshell, most senior politicians are utterly terrified of causing 'offence'.

For the Left, the resort to identity politics has been a disaster, for it has shifted the focus from broad-based campaigning and organising to advance the interests of the working class as a whole according to the things that united them – a desire for a secure job, decent pay, pensions, housing, and so on – and towards narrow, isolated battles around the unique attributes of a given group. It is a sad reality that much of today's Left seems interested less in fighting for 'the class' and more in pursuing struggles according to the biological characteristics, sexual orientation or religion of a particular section of society. Little wonder that Britain's working-class movement is increasingly fragmented and disjointed.

The whole philosophy of identity politics demands that minority groups be seen as inherent victims – regardless of the material circumstances of individuals – and that it must fall to society's progressives to protect them from the oppression of the so-called 'privileged' majority. This all seems to be a world apart from the self-organisation in times past of minority groups in an effort to overcome prejudice and fight for their rightful place in a cohesive and tolerant society. Rather, in actively promoting the separateness of these groups and seeking to amplify and celebrate difference for its own sake – as though their unique characteristics were virtuous in their own right and made them worthy of preferential political treatment – it is an ideology that conflicts sharply with the values of those who led past struggles against discrimination, including arguably the finest among them, Martin Luther King, who famously spoke of his desire to live in a society that judged a man not by the colour of his skin but by the content of his character.

The predominance of middle-class metro-liberals, progressives and graduates across so much of today's Left has unquestionably been a key factor in the emergence and entrenchment of identity politics. It was perhaps inevitable that as these cohorts – possessed as they were of greater wealth and status than most working-class people could hope for – took control of the movement, so its priorities would shift from the bread and butter concerns over employment, growth, living standards and security, and towards more cultural and sociological issues.

But for others among these groups – and particularly younger graduate-types – there is perhaps another explanation. Once upon a time, a university degree and entry into a professional, well-remunerated occupation would allow a graduate to telegraph his own intellectual abilities, material standing and general worthiness – and, in doing so, to differentiate himself from the working class. Nowadays, however – largely as a consequence of an economic landscape which hinders material advancement, as well as the upsurge in the numbers across all classes going to university – many struggle to demarcate themselves from the working class in any material sense, and hold out little hope of being able to do so in the future.

So displaying an educated and militant progressiveness in cultural and sociological issues, and doing so in a way that enables them to be identified as a member of a group of similarly enlightened people, has, for those who have given up on material advancement (or simply don't care about it), become an alternative method of distinguishing themselves from the less-educated masses, while still showing that they remain on the 'right' side of politics. Thus, expressions of wokeness can be seen as something of a status indicator as well as a political stance.

For members of the various identity groups themselves who happen to enjoy some degree of wealth or privilege, identity politics provides an opportunity – one that many seem only too willing to take – to posture as though they don't possess these things, thereby allowing them to win favour within a movement that increasingly elevates victimhood and rights over agency and duty. This in turn has meant that the concept of organising across the labour movement in pursuit of winning advances for the common good seems to have been supplanted by an attitude that persuades individuals, regardless of their personal circumstances, to see themselves as victims through being a member of a particular marginalised group, and then to expect some benevolent middle-class saviours or the state to come to their aid. It is, ultimately, a deeply paternalistic and disempowering process.

### Whiteness as original sin

When it comes to the question of whiteness, it is the woke Left, rather than the likes of me, who seem to have the obsession. The whole divisive concept of 'white privilege' – meaning that, even if their social or economic circumstances are the same, a white person will, thanks to other historical or cultural factors, always enjoy some kind of unearned benefit over a non-white – has emerged with the growth of identity politics. It's a theory that has been used as a stick by various woke liberals and progressives to beat certain cohorts of white people – usually working-class or suburban middle-class, socially conservative, patriotic and, more latterly, Leave voters.

There is, of course, merit in the argument that, all other things being literally equal, a person of colour stands a greater chance than a white person of experiencing mistreatment on the basis of race. Fundamentally, though, the concept of white privilege is entirely unhelpful because it ignores the crucial issue of class, which, for the Left, ought surely to be the primary consideration.

If a black person, for example, enjoys some degree of status and class privilege, then the lack of privilege associated with his skin colour becomes far less of a problem. Conversely, someone who is white but unemployed or homeless, and with limited means in the way of money or skills to remedy his situation, can hardly be said to tangibly benefit from any sort of inherent privilege, let alone one based on his skin colour.

That there is a range of factors, therefore, influencing the life chances and social status of black and white alike means that the theory of white privilege remains (or at least ought to remain) largely an academic one. Class privilege, or lack of it, surely matters above anything else. How many people, for example, given the choice, would sooner be a poor, uneducated white person than a wealthy, educated black person in today's Britain?

A Left that seeks to immerse itself in this divisive stuff – which makes working-class people feel as though they are guilty of some kind of original sin on account of their skin colour, rather than tries to build unity across the class – is a Left that is doing far more harm than good.

The theory of white privilege has, naturally, been swallowed whole by large parts of our liberal establishment and by corporations, who will engage in all manner of self-flagellation to demonstrate contrition for their sins. It is this thinking, no doubt, which has led many institutions and firms to develop initiatives specifically excluding white people.

In 2018, for example, the BBC was looking for a trainee multi-media journalist to work on its Radio 1 *Newsbeat* show.[1] In its advert for the job, the corporation made clear that whites should not apply: it wished to provide a pathway into journalism specifically for a person of colour. What this meant, of course, was that a young, poor, white working-class person living in a deprived part of Britain who may have possessed genuine talent and dreamt of a career in journalism was excluded from applying on the grounds that he was somehow more advantaged than, say, a middle-class Asian who had been to university and was the offspring of wealthy parents.

Yet a cursory examination of our media and entertainment industries – witness, for example, BBC television dramas – would suggest that the white working class is, if anything, more under-represented than most other groups.

None of this is to argue that we need to start waging a culture war on behalf of the white working class; rather it is to make the case that we need to halt the culture wars being prosecuted on behalf of other identity groups.

## Competing priorities

It is no coincidence that, as identity politics has taken root, the preoccupation of much of the Left has been in pursuing causes which embody it. Thus, the modern Left, including large elements of the Labour Party, will devote a wildly disproportionate amount of time and resources – almost to the point of obsession – campaigning on identitarian causes and, frankly, not enough on speaking about other issues that really matter to millions of ordinary voters.

An example is gay rights. Those who disagree that gay and lesbian people should be able to live their lives free from prejudice are, thankfully, fewer and fewer. Nonetheless, for many voters, gay rights remains a fringe issue: they understand there is a place for it; they believe gay and lesbian people must be protected from persecution; but it isn't at the top of their everyday agenda, and they don't think it should be so for politicians either. Yet among politicians and activists on the Left, it remains a first concern, such that they talk about the issue far more frequently than the average voter does – all of which serves to reinforce the perception of a Left with a different order of priorities to those whom it seeks to represent.

In some cases, the development of divisions between distinct identity groups has been an entirely deliberate act. For instance, the attempt by parts of the modern Left, for wholly cynical purposes and much related to Brexit, to pitch young people against old was all part of the ploy to present the former as enlightened and progressive (and, of course, mainly pro-EU), and the latter as bigoted and xenophobic (and mainly pro-Brexit). The term 'gammon' – a pejorative tag aimed at a particular group of older, white, male voters – entered the political lexicon during the Brexit convulsions. The message was clear: older people were the problem.

This was all of a piece with a wider fetishisation of youth over recent years by modern Leftists who see teenagers as allies in the fight against the forces of reaction. No matter that the young will usually possess nothing of the life experience or knowledge of more mature voters, their cheerleaders will attribute to them the gifts of great wisdom and foresight, and make political demands, such as 'Votes at 16', on their behalf. The truth, of course, is that such demands are just a form of gerrymandering: unable to win support for their ideas among a majority of adults, frustrated modern Leftists instead seek to change the rules of the electoral system to get their way.

But this approach fails to recognise the simple reality that many young people, regardless of how they might have voted on Brexit (and it's worth remembering that just under a third of 18–24 year olds voted Leave[2]), are ultimately motivated by the same desires as their elders: the opportunity of a decent job, affordable housing, secure family life, and so on. This means that while they are likely to be more socially liberal and individualistic now (even if, for example, they have poorly paid and insecure jobs), they will in many cases adopt a more communitarian and – dare it be said – conservative outlook once (or, given the current economic landscape, *if*) they acquire these things and realise they are worth defending. That's why the crude argument that the country is inexorably on a path to becoming yet more liberal and progressive as a consequence of older voters dying off and younger ones maturing is so wrong-headed. Rare is the person who maintains consistent political views throughout his entire life.

The attempt, then, by some on the modern Left to

co-opt certain identity groups as ideological allies is often rooted in a patronising assumption that everyone within those groups must inevitably agree with them and always will. Their approach to the Muslim community is further evidence of this. Many on today's Left think of Muslims as some kind of homogeneous block, all of them victims of oppression and prejudice by the state and media and the army of 'gammon', and thus certain to be partners in the struggle for progressive values. But far from viewing themselves in this way, or merely as voting fodder for our liberal elites, many Muslims hold what might be considered a profoundly socially conservative and patriarchal worldview which conflicts violently with the precepts of cosmopolitan liberalism and the 1960s-inspired cultural revolution.

This approach further betrays a major contradiction in the modern Left's approach to cultural politics. On the one hand, it enthusiastically promotes the liberation of the individual through personal autonomy and self-gratification – often no matter the consequence – while opposing 'repressive' or 'authoritarian' laws, institutions and mores, and the concepts of self-restraint, duty and self-sacrifice often associated with these things. On the other hand, it is, when it suits, only too willing to see minority groups as uniform slabs, devoid of individuality – and then to enlist these groups as collective allies even when many within them hold a completely conflicting worldview.

These contradictions mean that when, for example, Muslim parents protest against the teaching of LGBT equality in schools, as they did in Birmingham in 2019, much of the Left finds itself afflicted by a cognitive dissonance and isn't sure which way to turn.

## *Why multiculturalism has failed*

Similar contradictions can arise on the Left as a consequence of its enthusiasm for state-sponsored multiculturalism. Support for such a policy is still broadly considered the conventional wisdom on the Left – as indeed it is these days across most of the political spectrum – but there are pockets of dissent which are beginning to question whether multiculturalism is quite the progressive and enlightened idea it is cracked up to be.

At its core, a policy of multiculturalism rests on the active promotion of separation and difference – the idea that the distinctive biological or communal characteristics of identity groups should be accentuated and seen as virtuous in themselves. Moreover, within this philosophy there is no role for the state in giving priority to a particular cultural tradition. 'All cultures must be winners', could be the motto – except that, as you might expect, the main purveyors of this brand of identity politics – again the middle-class liberal and graduate types who dominate today's Left – are happy to sneer at anything that could be associated specifically with white working-class culture.

The brutal reality is that the ideology of multiculturalism, far from bringing unity and harmony across our nation, has given us divided communities and monocultural ghettoes in which particular ethnic or religious groups live parallel lives to many of their compatriots. And it is, frankly, pointless and dishonest to argue otherwise. The evidence is all around us. In the end, multiculturalism isn't, as some well-heeled progressives seem to view it, just about having a wider selection of fashionable restaurants on the high street.

The Left made a fatal error when it opted for the salad bowl over the melting pot. In doing so, it discouraged and disincentivised assimilation, and drove wedges between communities. And we cannot – at least not without consequence – continue to ignore the atomisation and fragmentation that marks some of our communities as a result, nor to candidly discuss why it has happened and how it might be put right.

None of this is to say that we should not defend with every fibre the right of individuals to live the lives they wish to live within the parameters of the law, to dress and eat as they like, and to worship the god they choose. Such liberties are central to a free society and any attempt to curtail them must always be resisted fiercely. Anyone who would entertain the thought that a fellow human should suffer ill-treatment on account of such things as his race or faith has no place in civilised society.

But rather than support a policy that emphasises and celebrates separateness, the Left must turn its hand to fostering the deepest (though nonetheless *unforced*) social and cultural consensus across our communities, not only in the interests of bringing estranged people together, but also because, once again, the maximum class-based unity is essential in the struggle to advance the interests of the working class. Yet, as it is with other forms of identity politics, class is relegated to a sideshow in the pursuit of multiculturalism.

Too often, the champions of multiculturalism will conflate criticism of their policy with racism, as though it were impossible to be both a multi-racialist and an opponent of multiculturalism. That is a nonsense, of course. They are also repelled at the idea of there being an accepted dominant culture within British society, and one that is prioritised in public policy. Such a thing, they aver, would be chauvinistic and exclusionary.

Yet there is no reason why a nation cannot defend an established and dominant culture while remaining civilised and free. Japan, for example, appears no less happy, prosperous or safe for its deep cultural homogeneity. In fact, it is arguably more so.

A fact often lost in the debate is that significant parts of Britain remain largely untouched by multiculturalism. The residents of these places might therefore be forgiven for being slightly irritated at statements from political leaders – usually made from their roost in the cosmopolitan cities – that seek to portray the nation as a whole as multicultural. It's a representation that, in fact, conflicts with the reality of many.

We also hear regularly the statement that 'diversity is our strength'. This, however, amounts to little more than rhetoric. The uncomfortable truth is that – as some commentators have begun to realise – the more diverse a society, the weaker the sense of social solidarity among its citizens is likely to be. Support for such things as redistribution of wealth through the tax system and the funding of a welfare state and public services rely heavily on there existing within a society sufficient levels of cohesion, reciprocity and mutuality. Thus, the greater the social and cultural distinctions, the less willing will be its members to sustain these things. Social solidarity – socialism itself – is built around what is shared, not what differentiates. Wishing or pretending that this were not the case, or trotting out unconvincing platitudes, ultimately serves nobody.

There has developed a feeling within many white working-class communities, not without justification, that their own traditions and culture are somehow illegitimate and must be suppressed, while they are simultaneously expected to embrace cultural diversity more generally and celebrate the particular traditions of others. Eric Kaufmann, professor of politics at the University of London, has described this as 'asymmetrical multiculturalism'.[3] It is again rooted in the belief among enlightened progressives that the white working class is guilty of some kind of original sin for which penance is owed.

When, as I recounted in the previous chapter, my friends and neighbours in Barking and Dagenham expressed their anxieties over cultural erosion, they were told by the liberal and cultural elites (whose own social circles always seem to comprise a remarkably homogeneous network of fellow middle-class educated types) to stop being nativist and embrace the new diversity because it was good for them. I am certain, however, that these same elites would never dream of venturing into, say, a Muslim or Amish or ancient Chinese community and insist they open themselves up in the name of diversity. Neither would they dare to suggest to a Native American or Indigenous Australian that their fears over cultural erosion were misplaced and nativist. But the white working class in Britain seems fair game.

### The gender identity madness

Perhaps the most contentious area of debate when it comes to identity politics – one that has led to a mini-civil-war on the Left and seen a disturbingly high-handed approach by the police – is transgenderism. In 2017, the Tory government floated the idea of reforming the Gender Recognition Act to allow individuals to legally self-declare as the opposite gender without having to go through a medical process. With this proposal, a bomb was detonated, and what had previously been an obscure debate suddenly exploded into the mainstream.

Immediately, many on the modern Left threw their weight behind the proposal. It was all in keeping with the aim of fighting for equality and against prejudice, they argued. If you weren't on board, you were a 'transphobe'.

But they hadn't reckoned with a small but determined group of women – many of whom were themselves of the Left – who saw it rather differently. These women, some of them stalwarts of campaigns against prejudice stretching back years, foresaw trouble. The hard-won victories that had delivered better rights for women – giving them dignity and security in the workplace and public spaces, for example – were in danger of being undermined. If a man could declare himself a woman without any real checks and balances, what might be the implications?

In making their argument, they pointed to real-life examples of how the desire of some authorities to indulge the demands of men identifying as women had already carried profound implications for the safety of the latter, such as the case of convicted rapist Karen White, formerly Stephen Wood, who had been placed in a women's prison and, while there, sexually assaulted two fellow inmates.[4]

There were other, more technical, questions, such as whether men identifying as women would be factored in when calculating the gender pay gap or crime figures.

More pertinently, wouldn't affording men the right to identify as women so easily effectively eradicate the concept of womanhood altogether (or, indeed, manhood in reverse cases)? How would the word 'woman' even be defined in future if being one had no basis in objective truth but were instead reduced to a mere personal feeling?

These real, justified concerns could not be explained

away by recourse to slogans about 'fighting for equality'.

As the debate intensified, the campaign to defend women's sex-based rights began to make a real impact. This meant, in turn, that those behind the campaign found themselves subjected to the most appalling abuse and harassment by an increasingly militant trans lobby.

The police invariably took the side of the militants. Merseyside Police, for example, confirmed it was investigating after 'Liverpool Resisters' – a women's rights' group – pasted stickers displaying the message 'Women don't have penises' on statues on Crosby beach. The Labour mayor of Liverpool pledged to 'remove [the] stickers and work with the police to identify those responsible'.[5] So here were the local constabulary and a senior local politician co-operating in their pursuit of a group of women whose only transgression had been to state a simple biological fact.

In a similar case, Thames Valley Police pledged to hunt down the culprits after stickers displaying messages identical to those found in Crosby, as well as others such as '"Woman". Noun. Adult human female', began appearing around Oxford. The force's investigating officer declared: 'Behaviour like this is not acceptable, and we take incidents of this nature very seriously.'[6]

Then there was Maya Forstater, a tax expert who was sacked by a think-tank for tweeting her view that people cannot change their biological sex.[7] She argued that she should not be compelled to use pronouns to describe individuals who were not of the sex designated by those pronouns. Forstater lost her employment tribunal claim for discrimination. In his ruling, the tribunal judge stated:

the Claimant is absolutist in her view of sex and it is a core component of her belief that she will refer to a person by the sex she considered appropriate even if it violates their dignity and/or creates an intimidating, hostile, degrading, humiliating or offensive environment. The approach is not worthy of respect in a democratic society.[8]

The judge seemed to be arguing that democracy depends upon citizens being compelled to say things they know in their hearts and heads to be false. But such an approach is surely the very antithesis of a free and democratic society, and more in keeping with the nature of the most totalitarian regimes.

Harry Miller, from Lincoln, was a retired police officer and vocal opponent of the proposal to introduce gender self-declaration, regularly taking to Twitter to express his concerns. After retweeting a limerick in support of his view, he found himself the subject of an investigation by Humberside Police. Mr Miller said he was contacted by a 'community cohesion officer' from the force, who told him, 'You've committed no crime, but we need to check your thinking.' Officers also visited him at his place of work. Needless to say, Mr Miller's actions were recorded as a 'hate incident'.[9]

Though still relatively tiny, the number of people declaring themselves 'non-binary' – meaning they identify as neither male nor female – has increased in recent years, probably as a by-product of the general growth in transgenderism. Those doing so will often insist that others should in future refer to them using only neutral pronouns such as 'they', 'them' and 'their'. One such was the award-winning singer and songwriter Sam Smith, who came out as non-binary in 2019. Needless to say, the entire media and cultural establishment immediately fell into line and, in accordance with Smith's wishes, began using neutral pronouns when referring to him, doubtless petrified of being accused of the offence of 'misgendering'.

Some may argue, in defence of this practice, that it is simply about displaying good manners and ultimately harms no one. But, as usual, that isn't where it ends. For the demands have become ever more unreasonable, going beyond an expectation that individuals show personal politeness and becoming an insistence that the law intervene and punish anyone who dares not comply. And, as we shall see, the law is increasingly responsive to demands that causing offence be in some way proscribed.

Suddenly, it isn't enough to say that individuals should be able to live as they choose free from persecution. Instead, society is, in such cases, expected to set aside everything it has known about custom, language and scientific truth to accommodate the wishes of a relatively tiny number of people.

### Free speech imperilled

All of this points to a society that has taken an Orwellian turn. It is barely an exaggeration to say that free speech is slowly dying in Britain. As with the erosion of many freedoms, people won't realise it is gone until it is too late. This may be because, outwardly at least, our country still bears all the characteristics of a free and functioning democracy. We don't experience a secret police force knocking on our doors in the middle of the night, or the suppression of newspapers, or laws censoring criticism of the government.

But what we do have is an increasingly suffocating and repressive culture that demands certain views be left unexpressed. Or, at least, anyone who does express them must be willing to sacrifice his reputation among polite society, and, in the worst cases, his livelihood too.

It cannot be doubted that much of the responsibility for this gradual but nonetheless very deliberate subversion of one of our most ancient of liberties lies with the liberal left. For it is the liberal left whose philosophy, rooted in the precepts of the 1960s cultural revolution, now dominates throughout many of our public and educational institutions and much of our media, and which sets the rules for what passes as acceptable opinion. And, for all its waxing lyrical about tolerance and diversity, it is the liberal left which exhibits an uncompromising ruthlessness when those rules are breached. Tolerance and diversity in everything but opinion seems to be its maxim.

The voicing of opinions that don't accord with the liberal consensus may still – just about – be permissible for those with no public standing, though even for these individuals it is probably safer that such views are aired only behind closed doors or when among friends. But any public expression of an unfashionable belief by someone in a position of authority, or with a modicum of prominence, is likely to be met with a fierce assault on that person's character, demands that he apologise or resign (or both), a social media storm, and an appeal to media organisations to deny him any future platform. Very probably, too, the person's employer will issue a statement distancing itself from his views and assuring the public that those views do not represent the organisation.

There was a time when those opposing the arguments of others would say, 'I think you are wrong', or 'I disagree with you.' But, today, it is increasingly common to hear instead the commandment: 'You mustn't say that.'

Over recent years, an entire industry has grown up around the taking of 'offence'. It isn't enough for some on the modern Left to disagree with alternative opinions;

they must also claim to have been 'offended' that the opinion was expressed in the first place.

But even if a particular opinion does happen to cause offence to someone, what of it? History tells us that progress has often been achieved only because particular individuals were courageous enough to express unorthodox beliefs – beliefs that at the time may have caused offence to many of their peers. Place certain topics beyond debate and the opportunity for society to scrutinise itself, make advancements or learn from its mistakes is much reduced.

I do not argue that one should be free to, as the old metaphor goes, shout 'Fire!' in a crowded theatre, or incite violence, or make libellous statements against another. Neither do I contend – although I don't suggest it should be illegal – that one should set out to cause offence gratuitously, as there is no virtue in hurting the feelings of a fellow human for no reason other than that you can. But if someone chooses to take offence because another has expressed a genuinely held political or moral belief, then the problem lies surely with the person taking offence, not the person offering his view.

For many on the modern Left, saying 'I am offended' or 'That is offensive' is enough to warrant the argument being terminated at that point. They consider it a trump card in debate – one that instantly renders the other person's position irrelevant, regardless of its merits. But – and here's the twist – the expressions of outrage by these individuals are rarely genuine. Usually, those claiming to be 'offended' are not in reality demonstrating their own hurt and anger; rather they are doing so on behalf of others whom they believe ought to be offended. It's a kind of vicarious indignation. And, what is more, they thoroughly enjoy manufacturing such uproar. Anyone who has ever been the subject of a Twitterstorm will know that the woke liberals who generate such fury take great satisfaction in egging each other on to ever greater levels of hysteria. It's like a form of solidarity between them: they will wait, ready to pounce, for each new instance of wrong-speak, and then rally their forces in pursuit of the perpetrator.

Moreover, those who are alleged to have said or done something offensive are expected to pay a heavy price even in cases where everyone knows it was not their intention to cause offence. When the Duke and Duchess of Sussex's first child was born in 2019, the well-known radio presenter Danny Baker tweeted the caption 'Royal baby leaves hospital' above an old black-and-white photograph of some High Society couple posing on the steps of an elegant building, with a chimpanzee, attired in a smart coat and bowler hat, between them. Baker's intention, he later explained – though it was pretty obvious even at the time – was to lampoon privilege. When, minutes after posting the tweet, Baker was informed that it might be interpreted as racist on account of the Duchess of Sussex's African-American heritage, he immediately deleted the tweet and apologised. No one seemed to doubt that Baker had not acted with racist intent, nor that his apology was sincere. But that wasn't enough.

The reaction was ferocious. Baker was quickly sacked by the radio station for which he worked – BBC Radio 5 Live – whose controller said in a statement: 'Danny made a serious error of judgement on social media last night, and it goes against the values we live and breathe on this radio station.'[10] Soon afterwards, it was reported that the Metropolitan Police were investigating the tweet. (The case was later dropped, though presumably only after a team of officers had spent valuable time establishing the facts and considering their options.) In a statement on Twitter, Baker said: 'I went to a file of goofy pictures and saw the chimp dressed as a lord and thought, "That's the one!" Had I kept searching, I might have chosen General Tom Thumb or even a baby in a crown. But I didn't. God knows I wish [I] had.' So Baker's crime was not to have demonstrated racism, or even intended it, but simply to have posted something that provoked cries of 'offence' by others and suggestions that some may merely *interpret* Baker's actions as racist – even though everyone seemed to accept they weren't. As ever, there was no slack to be cut in the frenzied mission to find examples of wrong-speak and publicly vilify offenders.

The irony in these types of cases is that the accusers, in their denunciations, often unwittingly display their own prejudice. It is likely that the vast majority of those who viewed Baker's tweet did not associate it with racism. Yet some, for reasons only they know, immediately saw the chimpanzee and thought of the Duchess of Sussex's African-American heritage. And these same individuals who upon spotting a chimpanzee thought 'black person' then presumed to accuse Baker of 'racial insensitivity'.

Baker was lucky enough to be an established and popular name in broadcasting. For a new and relatively unknown presenter, the episode would have been career-ending.

### *The tyranny of the woke slacktivists*

Those who foment these kinds of protests with a few taps on a keyboard or iPhone will often have had little experience of organising or campaigning against injustice in the real world. Many will not have taken part in marches or demonstrations, or been members of a political party or trade union, or have engaged in any real grassroots activity in support of a particular cause. But social media has given them the opportunity to publicly flaunt their woke credentials. By participating in a Twitterstorm generated in response to someone or something that has 'offended' them, they content themselves that they are somehow fighting for a better world.

This 'slacktivism' is the preserve of what have come to be known as 'virtue signallers' – people who think that joining a bandwagon of online rage, or sharing a hashtag or meme, or wearing a wristband promoting a charity or special cause, or publicly expressing a fashionable political or moral opinion, are substitutes for the hard yards of organised political struggle. Again, there is a distinctly middle-class whiff about the whole thing, with expressions of wokeness acting as some kind of status indicator designed to hand the protagonist instant social kudos and differentiate him from the ranks of the horny-handed working class.

At its core, this phenomenon is also deeply illiberal and operates in tandem with efforts to invalidate and silence alternative opinions. Again, it is rooted in the belief of those behind it that their arguments are so obviously correct and unanswerable that there must be no room for dissent. There is a certainty about their rightness – as though they have reached their conclusions through some kind of objective discovery, rather than via the normal mechanisms of discussion and disagreement. This causes them to see themselves as members of some enlightened in-group whose progressive views make them Inherently Better People.

The prominent campaigning outfit 'Stop Funding Hate' is a prime example of this way of thinking. This group publicly names and shames businesses that advertise in certain newspapers with whose editorial line it disagrees. The objective is to encourage consumers to boycott these businesses until they agree to pull their adverts. The group claims that the newspapers it targets use 'hate and division to drive sales'.[11] But, of course, these newspapers are exclusively of a conservative persuasion and, in some cases, take a robust stance on issues such as immigration or are otherwise not in step with fashionable opinion on social or moral issues. Liberal newspapers, some of which can be every bit as hostile in their language towards individuals and causes they oppose, are left alone. It is plain, therefore, that Stop Funding Hate is less about preventing the spread of 'hate', and more about stifling opinions with which it disagrees.

The group presents itself, naturally, as principled and ethical. But, in truth, it is an example of how this type of virtue signalling can carry deeply sinister undertones. Ultimately, Stop Funding Hate is willing to see businesses go to the wall as a consequence of a boycott – with the loss, potentially, of many jobs – just to halt the dissemination of views it doesn't like. Such groups need to be resisted if we are serious about defending a free press. As it is, however, a number of companies have capitulated to the group's demands – some releasing craven statements of contrition for having ever placed advertisements in such newspapers in the first place. It is likely in many cases that the decision of these companies was driven less by a fear that a boycott would actually be effective than by a desire to avoid bad publicity. It's a prime example, though, of the chilling effect of caving in to a small and vocal group of unrepresentative activists crying 'hate'.

The word 'hate' as it appears in the group's name is, of course, a misnomer. 'Hate' is one of those words that over recent years have, for political purposes, been redefined so wildly as to bear little resemblance to their true meaning. Thus, we are constantly told by liberal commentators and politicians that Britain is bedevilled by 'hate'. One tactic of these individuals is to weaponise any reported rise in so-called hate crime. Thus, after the EU referendum vote, they would seize upon data showing any increase in such crime and portray it as indicative of Britain's descent into wretchedness.

Yet, there is no sustainable evidence to suggest that Britain is growing more hate-filled. While it is true that official statistics over recent years show an increase in hate crime, the Home Office, when releasing the figures, caveats them heavily each time by explaining that the rise is 'thought to have been driven by improvements in crime recording' and that 'growing awareness of hate crime is likely to have led to improved identification of such offences'.[12] To make matters more complicated, today's police are required to record all 'hate incidents'. These are incidents in which *no crime has actually been committed*, but someone has merely perceived the actions of another to be motivated by hostility or prejudice based on disability, race, religion, transgender identity or sexual orientation. Such incidents may involve little more than an online insult or the telling of an 'offensive' joke.[13] And, of course, modern police leaders, ever willing to ingratiate themselves with liberal opinion, have met the challenge of tackling 'hate' with enthusiasm. Considerable resources seem to be given over to flaunting the 'progressive' credentials of local constabularies, with police bosses regularly using social and other forms of media to demonstrate the wokeness of their organisations.

As ever, though, the distance between the policing of the streets and the policing of the mind is but a short step. In September 2018, South Yorkshire Police tweeted: 'In addition to reporting hate crime, please

119

report non-crime hate incidents, which can include things like offensive or insulting comments, online, in person or in writing. Hate will not be tolerated in South Yorkshire. Report it and put a stop to it #HateHurtsSY.' The message seemed clear: write or say something that someone else finds insulting, and we might be knocking on your door.

## Debasing our language

'Hate' has, along with 'racist', 'fascist', 'far-right' and 'Nazi', been the subject of the most grotesque kind of word inflation. The ubiquity of these terms in political discussion, particularly on social media, and the manner in which they are thrown so casually at opponents, has rendered them almost meaningless.

There was a time when 'racism' was understood to mean the demonstration of hostility or ill-treatment towards someone on account of his race. Now it can mean anything. Those who are liable to find themselves labelled with the 'racist' tag include anyone from opponents of uncontrolled immigration to individuals who display the flag of St George on their homes or cars.

Until fairly recently, the terms 'far-right' and 'fascism' also referred to something quite definite: between them, they signified skinheads, the National Front and BNP, a penchant for the Third Reich, white supremacism, extreme nationalism, a one-party state headed up by a supreme leader, the suppression of dissent, antipathy for democracy and pluralism, state domination over vast areas of national life, and so on. Now, through over-use and wilful misuse, these terms have become utterly debased, to the extent that some on the modern Left will think nothing of applying them to mainstream Tory politicians or conservative newspapers or the Brexit Party or Donald Trump supporters or, in fact, anything or anyone they find objectionable.

So little resemblance does their image of Britain bear to reality, it is impossible to take seriously the regular warnings of these individuals about the advance of the far-right and fascism. And such exaggeration isn't limited to fringe voices; on the contrary, mainstream figures are guilty of it. For example, when the House of Commons agreed to hold a general election in 2019, Labour shadow cabinet member Dawn Butler tweeted: 'The general election has just been called. This isn't a normal election. It is the fight of our lives to save our country from the far right.'[14] To the uninitiated, Butler's alert may have constituted a portent of a Britain besieged by jackboots and swastikas rather than the prospect of a government containing figures such as Sajid Javid and Priti Patel.

Butler isn't alone in the Labour Party. In fact, the party has more widely succumbed to such hysteria. Just a month prior to Butler's tweet, a delegate from Tooting in south London got to the rostrum at the party's annual conference – I was there – and, to loud cheers and applause, described Brexit as a 'far-right project'.[15]

Sometimes, prominent voices on the liberal left are oblivious to the contradictions in their own arguments. For example, in October 2019, *Guardian* columnist Andy Beckett penned a piece entitled 'Britain was complacent about the far right. Now it's out in force.'[16] In it, he recalled that the leader of the British Union of Fascists, Oswald Mosley, was banned by the BBC for over thirty years, and bemoaned that it was hard to imagine such a ban being imposed on a 'big far-right figure' today: 'Nigel Farage . . . has been a panellist on BBC One's Question Time 33 times . . . Boris Johnson [has] adopted

the boot-boy phrases and demagoguery of the far right.'
The implication was clear: Farage and Johnson were
modern-day Mosleyites and should be subjected to the
same degree of censorship as Mosley was.

Aside from the fact that, whatever one thinks of their
politics, neither Farage nor Johnson – both of them
instinctive small-state libertarians – could reasonably be
described as 'fascists', those such as Beckett (and there
are many of them on the modern Left) who demand that
political opponents be silenced in the name of anti-fascism
appear not to see any trace of irony in their position.

After the EU referendum, it was not uncommon
to witness demands from some of the more militant
Remain supporters for prominent Leave campaigners
to be banned from the airwaves or even hauled through
the courts for 'lying to the country'. Some went as far as
to suggest their fellow citizens be denied the vote unless
they could pass some intellectual test. Very rarely, if ever,
did such demands come from those on the other side of
the argument. Yet a myth was allowed to develop which
presented Remain as the pluralist, tolerant wing of the
debate and Leave as that of bigots and crypto-fascists.

The period after the referendum saw various campaigns established with the sole aim of stopping Brexit.
The public pronouncements of such groups often bordered on the neurotic. 'Bremain in Spain', for example,
is a group with a following of several thousands on
social media and comprised of British citizens living in
Spain. In March 2018, before attending an anti-Brexit
demonstration, one of its leading organisers tweeted:

> Today I told a Spanish friend that I was going to the UK
> to go to a demo. She asked what it was about and I said
> to fight against the fascist actions of the British govern-
> ment. Those words actually came out of my mouth. And
> that's when it sank in what #stopbrexit really is.[17]

In the 1930s, many Britons travelled to Spain to fight real fascists. Now, some were making the reverse trip to fight imaginary ones.

Ultimately, these types of outpourings from intolerant liberals are designed to demonise opponents and bully them into silence. They hope that by repeatedly branding something as a 'racist' or 'fascist' endeavour, or more generally as 'hateful', that thing will become delegitimised and anyone who supports it forced to pipe down.

### The tightening grip of the law

This whole toxic culture has been buttressed by the enactment over time of increasingly repressive laws designed to protect the sensibilities of various identity groups. These laws explain why the police are these days so confident about intervening in matters that once would not have concerned them.

Inevitably, one feeds off the other: as society becomes ever more conscious of the discreteness of identity groups, and nervous about causing offence, so the legislation – or at least the application of it – becomes more draconian. And as the law clamps down in ever harsher ways, so our sensitivity towards each identity group becomes still more heightened, leading to a reinforcement of the perception of their separateness. Alongside these laws sits wider legislation whose rather sinister aim seems to be to discourage the expression of offensive or unfashionable opinions more generally.

Taken together, these laws, wrapped up in such pieces of legislation as the Public Order Act 1986, Crime and Disorder Act 1998, Communications Act 2003, Criminal Justice Act 2003, Racial and Religious Hatred

Despised

Act 2006 and Equality Act 2010, have placed enormous power in the hands of the police and courts. Some of this legislation is undoubtedly praiseworthy and deserves to be kept, but certain sections of it – for example, those that make it a criminal offence to use words which, in certain circumstances, may be deemed 'insulting' or 'abusive', or to send a communication that is 'grossly offensive' – have the potential to be misapplied, and indeed have been.

What constitutes 'insulting', 'abusive' or 'grossly offensive' is, of course, highly subjective. And as our society has become more sensitive, so we have seen considerable mission creep, such that the authorities have used these powers in a way that is entirely disproportionate and, in some cases, borders on the totalitarian.

Those who have found themselves investigated by police (and, in some cases, prosecuted or convicted) under these laws, or otherwise had their conduct recorded as non-crime 'hate incidents', include Christian preachers opposing homosexuality or Islam; a stand-up comedian who posted a film to YouTube of his girlfriend's pug raising its paw in the manner of a Nazi salute; a teenager who quoted on her Instagram page a line from a song by US rapper Snap Dogg which contained the word 'nigga'; social media users who mocked the hairstyle of a suspected drug dealer featured in a police mugshot; the entertainer Jo Brand, who, in a deliberately provocative Radio 4 comedy programme joked about throwing battery acid at politicians (and immediately made it clear she was joking); the then Home Secretary, Amber Rudd, who gave a speech arguing that firms should favour British workers rather than recruit from abroad (she was reported to police by an Oxford professor); a Buckinghamshire pensioner who beeped her car horn at another driver (who happened to be black);

124

the columnist Rod Liddle, who wrote disparaging comments about the Welsh, prompting the police and crime commissioner for North Wales to attempt to have him prosecuted;[18] and an air passenger who joked – and it was very obviously a joke – on Twitter about blowing up an airport in frustration at flight cancellations.

One is not obliged to agree with any of the actions listed in these examples – or the doubtless numerous similar cases that never reach the media – to find the heavy-handedness of the authorities deeply troubling. Indeed, we may consider some of the actions repugnant. The point is whether the police and courts should have intervened.

In 2016, the mayor of London, Sadiq Khan, spent £1.7 million establishing a special police unit – branded by some as a 'Twitter squad' – dedicated to investigating offensive comments on social media.[19] And in 2017, *The Times* reported that 3,300 people had been arrested and questioned the previous year for comments they had posted on social media. This represented an increase of nearly 50 per cent over two years.[20]

In a high-profile case in 2018, six men were arrested (one was later charged) after burning a cardboard effigy of Grenfell Tower, with cut-out figures of residents hanging from the windows. One had taken a video of the incident, which, before long, found its way onto social media and went viral. Some of those present could be heard laughing and joking as the effigy burned.

There was a fierce public reaction. Many viewed the act, justifiably, as wicked and reprehensible. But on what grounds was it a police matter? That it was tasteless and offensive? If so, who decides what constitutes these things? Many people – including some of our most popular comedians – resort to what might be regarded as tasteless and offensive humour, but does anyone believe they should receive a knock at the door from the local constabulary? What, for example, separates Ricky Gervais, Frankie Boyle, Sacha Baron Cohen or Jimmy Carr – all renowned for causing offence with their caustic, un-PC jokes about the most sensitive of topics – from the Grenfell effigy burners? Is it merely a question of degree? In which case, who determines the point at which humour becomes 'unacceptable'? The police? The *Guardian*? Twitter?

Moreover, notwithstanding that the video inadvertently went viral, the effigy incident took place at a private party in someone's back garden, prompting some to ask whether it really ought to be the job of the authorities to pursue individuals for demonstrating a lack of taste and etiquette in their humour when gathered with friends in a private home.

Again, one isn't required to defend the 'joke' to believe that those responsible should not face the wrath of the law. Much better, surely, for the likes of the Grenfell effigy burners to be confronted with the contempt of decent-minded friends, family, neighbours and work colleagues than be hauled through the courts. But the police, as they so often do these days, used oppressive 'hate' laws to do the job instead.

### Politicians run for cover

Our politicians are not only largely indifferent to this new tyranny but, in many cases, have positively encouraged it. They increasingly seek to drive through controversial legislation and create an oppressive atmosphere that stifles the expression of unwelcome views – but then shield themselves from any anger that arises from their actions.

In the aftermath of the Brexit debate, for example,

when passions were running high, MPs came in for more direct criticism than many of them had been used to. The atmosphere in the House of Commons was often febrile. Some found themselves challenged in the street or heckled at public meetings. These protests were occasionally robust, but by and large peaceful.

A number of MPs, however – mainly, it has to be said, on the anti-Brexit side of the debate – were riled, and could often be found complaining on the media about this sudden new scrutiny. They demanded that words such as 'traitor' be struck from the political lexicon. They upbraided fellow MPs who referred to an anti-Brexit parliamentary bill as a 'surrender act'. They objected when Boris Johnson spoke of setting up a 'war cabinet' to deliver Brexit. Never mind a war cabinet, this was a war on metaphor.

In their efforts to insulate themselves from the heat of the debate, these MPs would often cite the terrible murder of their colleague Jo Cox – as though every Brexit activist were a potential killer.

To threaten MPs with violence or abuse them gratuitously is plainly wrong. But the right to challenge, criticise and satirise political representatives, to eyeball them and tell them they have let you down, to hold their feet to the fire and force them to experience the raw anger of the masses, is indivisible from democracy itself. It is these things that separate societies that value freedom and liberty from those that don't. In Britain, particularly, they are part of a centuries-old tradition, epitomised in the historical movements to give ordinary people a voice – the Levellers, the Chartists, the Peterloo martyrs, trade unions and suchlike – as well as in the poems of Shelley, the work of magazines such as *Punch* and *Private Eye* and TV programmes such as *Spitting Image*. There should be no room for the language police or courts in matters of political discourse and accountability.

When the Conservative MP Anna Soubry was confronted outside Parliament by a group of protestors over her role in the plot to stop Brexit, it was the prompt for over a hundred MPs to sign a letter demanding the police get tough with protestors.[21] The speaker of the house, John Bercow, went as far as to describe the actions of protestors as 'a type of fascism'. There was no recognition from these MPs that their own efforts to thwart the implementation of the decision of the British people were instrumental in creating such a feeling of anger and betrayal in the first place. Instead, they enlisted the help of Scotland Yard in deflecting the criticism.

One protestor called Soubry a 'Nazi' and 'traitor' during one of these encounters. It was an unpleasant, and unnecessary, thing to do. But, for this, he received an eight-week prison sentence (suspended for a year) and was banned from the area around Parliament.[22]

Of course, leading figures on the other side of the Brexit debate – Nigel Farage and Jacob Rees-Mogg, for example – would be regularly harangued and abused in the street by protestors, but rarely, if ever, was anything done about it. (Indeed, the Conservative MPs of the pro-Brexit European Research Group were compared to Nazis by Labour MP David Lammy, who then went on to argue that his comparison hadn't been strong enough.[23])

Similarly, ordinary Leave voters became accustomed, after the referendum, to being accused of facilitating 'fascism' and taking Britain back to the dark days of the 1930s. None of this seemed to matter to those on the other side of the argument demanding an end to 'divisive rhetoric'.

In another case, a Brexit supporter, Amy Dalla Mura, was prosecuted for 'harassing' Anna Soubry (her again).[24] Dalla Mura was what one might think of as a pain in the backside. She would often hang around when Soubry was giving media interviews or press conferences and heckle her. In the end, she was hauled through the courts and jailed for twenty-eight days. And, despite the fact that she was a declared candidate in Soubry's Broxtowe constituency in the 2019 general election, the court banned her from the constituency, thereby preventing her from running any meaningful campaign.

Dalla Mura's only crime was to be a persistent and irritating critic of a political representative whom she believed was responsible for subverting democracy. And, again, her treatment by the authorities stood in stark contrast to their leniency towards activists on the other side of the debate. For example, in the years after the referendum, the strident anti-Brexit activist Steve Bray was permitted to stand on College Green outside Parliament and constantly disrupt news broadcasts and interviews with pro-Brexit MPs by bellowing 'Stop Brexit!' at regular intervals.

In 2018, a church-going pensioner, Linda Banahan, emailed her local Conservative association to complain about the actions of her MP, Antoinette Sandbach, in voting to stymie Brexit in the Commons. 'I will do everything I can to make her treachery known', wrote Mrs Banahan. Sandbach replied directly – but only to inform her constituent that her email had been 'reported to the police'. This was too much even for the local constabulary, who confirmed that it was not intending to investigate the incident.[25]

It isn't only on Brexit that our elected representatives have sought to enlist the help of the authorities in deterring those holding a different view. In 2019, for example, the Labour MP Stella Creasy, who had been instrumental in driving through legislation designed to extend abortion rights to Northern Ireland, went as far as to demand the Metropolitan Police round up a peaceable group of pro-life protestors and run them out of her constituency.[26] She claimed that the protestors were guilty of 'harassing' her, whereas their only crime was to carry out a concerted and hard-hitting lobbying campaign against an elected legislator who, in their eyes, had helped to enact a pernicious law. No one was demanding Creasy have tea with her opponents – only that she respected their right to campaign for their view.

### The presumption of guilt

Our nation, then, is one in which many in positions of political influence increasingly seek to use legislation as an alternative to the challenge of winning the argument. We have, on what are deemed to be sensitive topics, become debate-averse and offence-averse. Our new national religion – let's call it 'liberal wokedom' – has infected large parts of our governing institutions, educational establishments, corporations and media, and we are run by a political class which, when confronted by the demands of any group or individual crying 'prejudice', 'offence' or otherwise demanding indulgence, is petrified of saying no and provoking a backlash.

It is this mindset that leads, for example, to the creation of 'safe spaces' in universities – institutions which ought surely to measure their success by how widely they expose their students to a range of competing viewpoints rather than how well they are insulated from them. And, naturally, the more the ears of students are protected against unfashionable or controversial opinions, the greater the anxiety and sense of outrage when they are confronted with one.

Not surprisingly, this whole approach has contributed to a culture of group-think that sees moral or political standpoints not as good or bad, or as matters to be debated civilly, but as legitimate or illegitimate – those which may be voiced and those which must remain unspoken. It is a destructive, coercive culture – one which seeks to intimidate opponents into conformity through fear of ostracism. And the reluctance of decent people to put their heads above the parapet means that those responsible for this culture feel confident about adopting ever more extreme positions.

The #MeToo movement is an example of this. In 2017, in the wake of a slew of sexual abuse allegations against the American film producer Harvey Weinstein, this movement took off across the globe. In Britain, news reports were suddenly filled with allegations of sexual impropriety against public figures, most notably politicians. Careers were placed in the deep freeze or terminated completely. In many cases, the allegations centred on little more than some cheesy sweet-talking, or what might once have been considered mild flirting. Often, the accused would deny the allegation vehemently. But the mere fact that it had been made was usually enough to destroy reputations. Actual evidence was deemed immaterial.

To be accused was to be damned. The whole phenomenon had the air of a medieval witch-hunt. Those who argued that we might perhaps reserve judgement on each allegation until some kind of investigation had taken place and the case for the defence had been heard were accused of defending sexual harassment and 'victim-blaming'.

This growing tendency to make immediate judgements

and demand swift retribution risks – indeed *is* – undermining some of our most ancient and fundamental liberties. One such is the presumption of innocence. This liberty, alongside the right to a defence and a fair hearing, provides a foundation stone upon which so much of our civilisation rests. But that stone is being slowly eroded by an intolerant mob desperate to signal their virtue and demonstrate they are on the side of society's 'victims'.

When, in 2014, Carl Beech claimed to be a past victim of a VIP paedophile network, making allegations of rape and murder against prominent figures across politics and the military, the Metropolitan Police didn't trouble to properly investigate his claims before describing them as 'credible and true'. Only later was a large-scale investigation – Operation Midland – established (at enormous financial cost) to examine the claims and pursue the alleged perpetrators. Beech's allegations led to the raiding of homes and the upturning of lives. But there was one small problem: Beech was a fraudster and fantasist, and his story a tissue of lies. Yet so eager had the police officers been to show they were on the side of 'victims', they immediately lent credibility to his claims and were ultimately complicit in the trail of devastation that ensued. Beech was later jailed for eighteen years.

The atmosphere around #MeToo and the Carl Beech allegations led a number of police forces to encourage victims of sexual abuse to come forward with their stories. These solicitations were often accompanied with the message: 'You will be believed.' In making this pledge, police may well have taken their cue from a 2014 report by Her Majesty's Inspector of Constabulary, who opined, quite remarkably, that 'the presumption that a victim should always be believed should be institutionalised'.[27] This statement violated at a stroke the longstanding principle of police impartiality and the convention that allegations be investigated without fear or favour. But these things mattered little in the face of the desire by police and their political masters to be seen as on the side of good against evil.

## *The intolerance of the 'tolerant'*

The result of this embrace of liberal wokedom, indulging the demands of a relatively small but vocal minority, is that our freedoms and liberties are increasingly being subverted and many of our traditions trashed. Moreover, the sheer rapidity of the ensuing political, social and cultural changes to our national life – changes that are often cemented in law – has left millions of ordinary citizens feeling like strangers in their own land – unwelcome, marginalised and disparaged.

To challenge the precepts of liberal wokedom is to leave oneself open to character assassination – sometimes to even risk arrest and prosecution. Traditional views which until very recently passed as perfectly acceptable, even mainstream, throughout society have, in some cases, been placed beyond legitimate debate.

Again, it isn't enough to believe that individuals should not be persecuted or ostracised for living their lives differently; there is instead the demand that everyone positively approve of the lifestyle choices of others.

As the proselytisers for liberal wokedom have begun to assert their dominance across our public life, so they have insisted the entire country convert. Values, opinions and principles to which many had held true all of their lives were expected to be jettisoned in the rush to enlightenment. And if some were unwilling, well, the law might have to intervene.

Take same-sex marriage. Many people in Britain hold to the traditional view that marriage ought to be between a man and a woman. Of course this position should not be beyond challenge, and those who advance it should not expect to never have to defend it in debate. But the sheer venom that is often directed at people for simply holding a belief that until fairly recently was regarded as the conventional wisdom throughout most of the country, including by many among our political and media elites, is deeply troubling.

Until 2013, same-sex marriage had no legal standing anywhere in the UK (though civil partnerships had been introduced in 2004). The reason for this was that most people, including those with their hands on the levers of power, believed that marriage between a man and a woman should be the only recognised form of the institution. There had not, over the years, been any sort of sustained campaign with mass appeal calling for same-sex marriage. Nonetheless, the Tory and Liberal Democrat coalition government of the time pushed through legislation paving the way for it.

Many people will argue that, in the interests of fairness and equality, enacting the legislation was the right thing to do – and that is of course a perfectly reasonable viewpoint. Yet some of these same individuals – especially those who are members of our dominant liberal class – immediately and doggedly refused to afford any understanding or respect to those who remained on the other side of the argument. The fact that, until the moment the legislation was laid before Parliament, the view in favour of traditional marriage was the established – and probably the mainstream – position throughout the land seemed to be irrelevant

to them. In their minds, once the legislation was introduced, it became year zero. The world had moved on
– very swiftly in this case – and anyone who wasn't
willing to move with it was a bigot.

There was no recognition that the millions on the
other side of the argument might find it a little challenging to accept a sudden new reality that just happened
to conflict with their own settled and well-established
culture and everything they had learned, known and
understood about marriage and family life.

Did these condescending liberals not stop to consider
that, if their arguments were taken to their logical conclusion, their characterisation of opponents of same-sex
marriage as bigots and reactionaries would have applied
to much of the population – including, perhaps, even
themselves – just a few years previous? It's almost as
if the very moment the Bill was introduced, society
suddenly became divided on the subject between the
enlightened and the ignorant. Did it not occur to them
that, whatever one's view on religion, it was undeniable
that the view of marriage to which they were suddenly
so hostile was one rooted in a belief system that was for
centuries the foundation stone upon which so much of
our nation's moral, legal and political framework was
constructed (and, to this day, happens to be the position
of the established church)?

No, they apparently considered none of this. There
was to be no honest debate, no careful transition
between the old and new, no attempt to gently per-
suade opponents, no acknowledgement that this, for
many, represented a profound cultural shift. Either you
embraced the change or you were a 'homophobe'.

None of this represents a plea to repeal the law on
same-sex marriage. Instead, it is an appeal to stop
the witch-hunt of those who have not accepted such

far-reaching change with the enthusiasm demanded of them by the liberal and cultural elites.

It is this whole mindset, this propensity to demonise and delegitimise and, in some cases, 'no-platform' those expressing alternative views, that must be challenged. Sooner or later the foot soldiers of the modern Left are going to have to wake up to the fact that millions of their compatriots do not think as they do and have no desire to be part of their enlightened in-groups. And that it is their own arrogance, belief in their own innate moral goodness and inability to comprehend that others may not agree with them, that is in no small part responsible for the rupture between the Left and so many working-class voters.

The Labour Party in particular is now filled with such people. It has become an organisation for social activists, students and middle-class urban liberals and progressives whose lives and priorities are usually very different from those of its one-time working-class base, and who have been complicit in the efforts to undermine freedom of expression through support for ever more draconian legislation and the creation of a culture in which the kind of traditional views still held by many among that base are seen as objectionable.

Labour today has virtually nothing to say to small-town and post-industrial Britain, the kind of places out there in the provinces which were once its mainstay. It is no longer the 'people's party', but the party for the woke, the Toytown revolutionary and Twitter.

The modern Left likes to preach to us the dictum of 'live and let live' and the need for mutual respect. But, in real life, it practises the complete opposite. While commanding us to accept without question the lifestyle choices and moral outlook of others, it is unwilling to afford the same courtesy to opponents. So anyone who continues in modern-day Britain to hold true to small 'c' conservative opinions – and there are many such people of all political persuasions across our country – becomes a target for attack. These individuals will not be shown respect or tolerance by the modern Left. More likely, they will be demonised and accused of being filled with 'hate'.

The Left's obsession with identity politics and wokeness, alongside its increasing hostility towards freedom of expression, has provided free kick after free kick to the populist Right, which always benefits more from culture battles than it does arguments over economics. The wonder is that anyone should then be surprised at the electoral consequences of all this.

The divisions that have broken out across our land over recent years are directly attributable to the suffocating, toxic atmosphere created by liberal and cultural elitists who have made a huge chunk of the population feel smeared and marginalised. The modern Left played a major part in taking a country that was – and, despite everything, still is – becoming more and more tolerant, and turned it into a place which is fighting a bitter culture war. And that is the greatest tragedy. It was a war that didn't need to be fought. But, having been started, it is unlikely to end any time soon.

# 4

# The Case for the Nation State

The world needs to de-globalise. Rapidly. Many of the social and economic tribulations experienced by Western nations in the past half-century – and, in particular, the eruptions of the past decade – can be traced directly to the weakening of the nation state, the erosion of national sovereignty and the delegitimising of national identity.

Where once there was broad consensus that a world comprised of independent nation states – responsible for making their own laws and running their own economies while promoting trade and co-operating in matters of security with their neighbours and partners – was the model most conducive to the maintenance of democracy, prosperity and peace, there is now increasingly the view (at least among many Western establishment figures) that the nation state has served its time, and that, in these days of deeper globalisation and interdependence, borders are redundant, national parliaments peripheral, and technocrats and business people best qualified to make the big decisions.

The attack on the concept of nationhood has been deliberate and purposeful. It has been spearheaded, for different reasons, by two groups of people who saw the

138

nation state as a roadblock to the implementation of their ideology.

First, the financial globalisers – those wedded to the precepts of neoliberal economics, namely the chiefs of the multinationals and banks, the international investors, and those with political power who support their ideology. This group, by definition, seeks ever greater reductions in regulation, less government intervention, lower taxes, fewer barriers to the movement of capital, a restraint on trade union power, more flexibility in the global labour market, the rolling back of the frontiers of the state – that is, within and between states – more power for supranational institutions and less for elected politicians of national parliaments. In short, they want access-all-areas in pursuit of higher profits and a greater share of the market.

This philosophy – which later became known as the 'Washington Consensus' – has its roots in the free market theories of Friedrich Hayek and Milton Friedman, and took hold as the post-war Keynesian economic consensus began to crumble around the mid-1970s. It places a requirement to restrain inflation at the centre of economic policy – even if that means rising unemployment and inequality – and sees austerity as the correct response to a recession. The market is seen as something near to infallible, and therefore to be fettered as little as possible.

These ideas define the very nature of globalisation. No wonder that those who believe in them see an independent nation state governed by elected politicians making their own laws and controlling their own economy in the national interest as a potential obstacle to their ambitions.

The second group are the political and cultural globalisers – the progressive purveyors of the kind of cosmopolitan liberalism which, as we have seen, has created a schism between ordinary working-class voters and their rulers in Britain, and explains the increase in support for populist movements and politicians throughout much of Europe and the United States. These people – often labelled (much to the irritation of some of them) 'citizens of nowhere' – are deeply suspicious of anything but the most dispassionate relationship with the nation state, associating patriotism with sentiments of chauvinism and dislike of Johnny Foreigner, and viewing it as a hindrance to their brand of internationalism, which is built around the notion of a liberal utopia unencumbered by such outmoded concepts as borders and sovereignty. They contend that sentiments of national pride and belonging must, by definition, be exclusionary, for it is simply impossible to hold such positive feelings about one's own country without harbouring hostility or ill-will towards others.

This group recognises that the nation state still performs a role in terms of governance but is happy to see its influence decline. It contends that, ultimately, no good can come from a world order that upholds the nation state as the optimal form of government at the highest level. It draws little distinction between the virulent nationalism which has undoubtedly scarred our world from time to time, and the benign patriotic attachment to country – and the associated simple desire to be governed by one's own people – still felt by millions of ordinary citizens. It sees the role of the nation state as little more than a functional one. That's why those in Britain who fall into this category were so jolted by the decision to leave the European Union. They viewed it as a victory for 'nativism' over progressivism and internationalism.

This group is itself divided in its view of globalisation.

Some don't especially like it but nonetheless eschew any suggestion that reinvigorating the nation state be a key part of any strategy to challenge it. Instead, they place their faith in protest movements – Extinction Rebellion, for example – and non-governmental organisations and charities, and seek to globalise the influence of these struggles and institutions, sometimes linking up with left-wing revolutionary elements (who in no sense could be classed as liberals but loathe the nation state equally) to that end.

Others, such as Blairites, 'Third Way' advocates and assorted self-declared 'centrists', have broadly accepted globalisation as the only show in town – and, in some cases, positively embraced it – arguing that the most elected politicians can hope to achieve is to harness it so far as possible to work in the interests of the masses. But this approach, however well-meaning, will always struggle to overcome the reality that, after more than three decades of globalisation in its current form, social and economic inequality remain entrenched, and that, rather than spreading wealth and opportunity, the new global economy has consolidated them in the hands of those at the top of the system. Indeed, it is a hallmark of so-called 'free markets' that the rules are shaped in the interests of those who held power and wealth to begin with, and the single global market is no different.

So, for example, according to the economist Branko Milanović, a specialist in income inequality, the world's top 1 per cent of earners saw their real incomes increase by around 40 per cent – a far higher increase than that experienced by virtually everyone else – in the period between 1988 and 2011.[1] Likewise, the *Global Wealth Report 2019* by the investment bank Credit Suisse found that all the world's US dollar millionaires, who accounted for 0.92 per cent of the adult population,

141

owned 44 per cent of all global wealth collectively – up from 34 per cent in 2000 – while the bottom half of wealth-holders owned less than 1 per cent.[2] Far from being immune to these inequalities in wealth, income and status, it is widely accepted that Western societies have, in some cases, suffered from the worst disparities.

Global free market policies, then, have systematically failed to deliver the very benefits that their cheerleaders promised us. Invariably, they have served the interests of the few over the many. And if there was any doubt at all that the 'market knows best' dictum was shaky, it ought surely to have been eliminated when the global financial crisis struck in 2007–8 and it became clear immediately that the market could not correct what it had caused.

When considering the damaging effects of neoliberal globalisation on developing countries – through, for example, the exploitation of cheap labour, the compulsory privatisation of public services and the decimation of local business at the hands of global corporations – as well as the harm caused to the environment through the plunder of natural resources and increased pollution, it is odd, to say the least, that anyone of the Left – especially those who consider themselves internationalists – should not regard the task of confronting it as all important. Yet many continue not to see it as a priority.

The nation state, however, though debilitated by everything the financial, political and cultural globalisers have thrown at it over recent decades, refuses to wither away. On the contrary, there are signs that it is making a resurgence.

The Covid-19 pandemic threw into sharp relief how a deepening interconnectedness and over-reliance on global supply chains (such as those providing personal protective equipment for health workers) had the capacity to undermine government responses to such crises, and demonstrated how the principle of a nation state supporting its own industrial and manufacturing base within the framework of a national economy was suddenly relevant again.

And there is surely now a compelling case for the British Left to embrace this resurgence. A radical and forward-thinking Left would make itself the driving force behind an urgent and necessary turning away from the injustices and short-termism inherent within the prevailing global economic order and towards more traditional and longer-term economic planning in which elected governments, willing to reclaim control over all aspects of macroeconomic policy and unashamedly representing the national interest, play a leading and essential role.

That would, for many, mean a profound rethink in their approach to questions of nationhood and national self-understanding. But if the Left's forces – such as the ranks of organised labour and social activism – are to be in any way effective in the task of ending the supremacy of market forces over ever greater areas of our lives, it must be understood that the nation state stands as a potential ally, not an adversary, in that struggle. Certainly not with a view to building some kind of socialist autarky or retreating into splendid isolationism, and neither because the nation state is a panacea for all our woes, but simply because, in the right hands, a nation state can still do much to mitigate the impact on its people of the worst excesses of globalisation. And a determined group of nation states working together to similar ends – though not within the context of neoliberal, supranational institutions like the EU – has the potential to act as an effective bulwark against the power of global capital on a much wider front.

That so many modern leftists have not grasped the value of the nation state in the struggle against the ravages of unrestrained global capitalism is a failure of epic proportions. In being so blinded by their prejudice against even the mildest forms of nationalism, they have severely hobbled their own efforts to counter the hegemony of the neoliberal ideologues and prevent them wreaking even more devastation.

## Democracy devalued

One of the major downsides of the weakening of the nation state is the devaluation of the vote. The advent of a global economy and the concentration of power and wealth in fewer and fewer hands has meant a corresponding increase in the influence of global corporations – whose leaders are not legitimated by the slightest democratic mandate, and indeed would never achieve one even if they were able to try – as well as those technocratic institutions, such as the International Monetary Fund and European Commission, whose role nowadays seems principally to uphold the system. This has meant, by extension, a sharp reduction in the influence and authority of elected governments.

In going with the flow and accepting as inevitable the onward march of globalisation, many Western governments and politicians appear to have concluded that they will only ever have an increasingly diminishing role in the affairs of their own country, as power and decision-making are outsourced to those who pull the strings at a supranational level in politics and commerce. They have reconciled themselves to the belief that, such is the nature of globalisation – with multinationals able to shift vast quantities of capital and even entire operations across the world with the minimum of impediment, and in so doing potentially destabilise national economies and cause massive economic and social disruption – it is better simply to acquiesce to the power of those multinationals rather than confront them. It is a form of economic blackmail: 'Do something we don't like', say the multinationals, 'such as raising taxes or improving workers' rights, and we'll take our money elsewhere.'

The global corporations know they have the whip hand over elected governments, and they will use this leverage to maximum effect. Faced with such a threat, many governments and parliaments are intimidated into ceding control of their own political and economic destiny, meaning that time and again the demands of the rich and powerful win out over those of the electorate. So firmly has this mentality taken hold that, even when they have been under no obligation to do so, British governments of all stripes have abrogated responsibility for running things and taking big decisions – from outsourcing of public services to giving power to bankers to set interest rates – on the assumption that business people and technocrats know best.

Much of the mainstream British Left stands guilty on this charge. Having declined to put up any serious resistance to the phenomenon of globalisation, and in concluding that the role of national governments in a globalised world in which market forces dominate must, by definition, be increasingly restricted, it has effectively taken the view that there is no alternative. And, thus, it finds itself trapped in an intellectual straitjacket, neither willing nor able to articulate a vision that might radically challenge the status quo.

Some may argue that the rise of Corbynism inside the Labour Party demonstrated a shift in thinking and a new willingness to tackle the prevailing global economic orthodoxy. Certainly Labour under Corbyn became much bolder in its readiness to confront vested interests, and spoke passionately of its desire to bring about a transfer of power and wealth to ordinary families. But it can hardly be said to have set out to challenge the over-arching global financial system under which much of the world lives. In truth, the radicalism of Corbyn's Labour was limited. Witness, for example, its lack of any com-mitment to restore the Bank of England to democratic control, or its consternation at the decision to leave the EU – one of the most powerful capitalist projects ever conceived – and its desperate attempts to reverse the result of the referendum.

The consequence of this draining away of author-ity from national governments and parliaments is the transfer of power more and more from the ballot box to the boardrooms of the multinationals, supported by the writ of supranational bodies. The scope for the demo-cratic process to act as a brake on the rapacity of the market and the ambitions of its exponents has been much diminished as a consequence of that market oper-ating in an increasingly uninhibited way across national boundaries. Globalisation can therefore be viewed as the domination of international capital and technocracy over the nation state and its citizens. In this way, it strips us of not just our economic power, but our political power too.

### Globalisation meets resistance

This erosion of national sovereignty and economic and political power goes a long way to explaining the rise in nationalist or quasi-nationalist movements across the West. For as the populaces of many countries have found themselves buffeted by the storms of global capital – witnessing the transfer abroad of local industry and jobs, and experiencing the rapid cultural and demographic changes that have come with liberalised immigration policies – so their sense of violation has increased. And when they tried to express their opposition through the democratic process, they discovered that most mainstream parties were signed up to the very system that had contributed to their misery.

Many on the Left have utterly misdiagnosed this phenomenon. They view it as having been born from an innate sense of national – and sometimes racial – superiority, or the naive masses having fallen for the demagoguery of populist leaders. Some talk of it as a threat to civilisation and warn of a return to the 1930s. In Britain, this attitude has been given undue legitimacy by the Brexit vote.

Yet, for the most part, these movements did not appear out of a clear blue sky and are not driven, as they were in the 1930s, by any sense of superiority, still less an aggressive expansionism or hostility towards other nations. On the contrary, they are defensive by nature and defined by a desire among ordinary citizens to defend what they have (or reclaim what they have lost) in the way of democracy, national self-determination, identity, and economic and cultural security, as well as a recognition that, if things are to change for the better, the peddlers of neoliberal globalisation – in many senses the architects of their plight – must be confronted.

A prime example of such a movement is the Gilet Jaunes in France. Formed in 2018 in protest at rises in the price of fuel and the cost of living under the centrist government of Emmanuel Macron, the movement quickly grew and expanded its demands to include greater economic justice – including a higher minimum

147

wage and an end to austerity – and a strengthening of democracy, such as by way of 'citizens' initiative referendums'. It was a genuine anti-globalisation movement, grassroots-led, comprised mainly of working-class people and infused with a patriotism redolent of historical French revolts. Every Saturday, thousands of protestors wearing their yellow vests and waving their tricolours would march through cities and towns across France, with each new demonstration designated the latest *Acte* in a drawn-out play.

Naturally, the European Left saw the movement as anything but inspiring and did its best to distance itself from the protestors. The Gilet Jaunes were just a bit *too* working class and rough around the edges. They were patriotic; they rejected the notion that an affluent urban elite knew what was best for them; they challenged the assumptions of cosmopolitan liberalism; and it was said that some of them weren't terribly keen on the European Union or mass immigration.

For its part, the voice of the British trade union movement, the Trades Union Congress (TUC), offered not a word in solidarity. Individual trade unions also remained silent. This wasn't because the protests were taking place outside their own territory. On the contrary, Britain's trade unions have frequently waxed lyrical about their 'internationalist' credentials, and are usually never slow to offer solidarity to workers abroad – such as those in Cuba or Venezuela – when they feel the need. But not the Gilet Jaunes. These particular workers were off-limits. Their ideas conflicted with the progressive, cosmopolitan, liberal worldview to which much of the movement in Britain today is wedded.

Its failure to back the Gilet Jaunes was the clearest indication of how the trade union movement in Britain had moved away from being rooted in the traditional values of the working class. How easy it would have been to issue words of encouragement, to take the short hop across the Channel and stand shoulder to shoulder with French workers fighting back against the establishment. But, no. The Gilet Jaunes waved national flags while they marched. So they were given a wide berth.

Some justified their stance with the claim that the Gilet Jaunes were supported by elements from the far-right. But, insofar as this was true, any protest movement for economic justice that attracts the support of so many millions of ordinary people across an entire nation will, by definition, appeal to some less savoury characters. This should not be seen as a reason to blacklist the entire movement.

Many modern leftists view the Gilet Jaunes and similar movements that have emerged across the West as inimical to the internationalist ideal. Such movements, they believe, are a presage of a world retreating into narrow nationalism and must be opposed. But these movements are, for the most part, not hostile to the principles of internationalism and pose no threat to their neighbours. Instead, their emergence was a reaction to the damage inflicted on communities by the new global market and can be seen as an attempt to seek refuge from the onslaught.

To conflate globalisation and internationalism is therefore an elementary but grave error, for the two are fundamentally different. But it's an all-too-common error on the Left, and one that probably further explains the aversion of many among its ranks to Brexit. The truth, of course, is that one can proudly uphold internationalist ideals while also being an implacable opponent of globalisation.

Indeed, it could be argued that the corralling of nations, often against the will of their people, into ever

closer political and economic union with others is likely
to retard the journey towards the deeper degree of
international co-operation that such integration seeks,
ostensibly at least, to bring about.

## *Turning the tide:*
## *challenging the power of global capitalism*

So is there a realistic alternative to the prevailing orthodoxy? Should neoliberal globalisation be seen as some
kind of unstoppable natural phenomenon, like the rising
of the tide and waxing of the moon? Must nation states
resign themselves to their ever-receding role in matters of international politics and commerce?

Surely anyone on the Left must start from the point
of recognising that, given the deleterious consequences
of the new global economy for many ordinary citizens,
there must be an alternative. The system has failed millions, subverted democracy, laid waste to communities,
industry and the environment, and created a race to the
bottom in terms of wages and standards. There must,
therefore, be a concerted pushback against it.

And this is where the nation state comes in. For, in the
absence of either an international socialist revolution –
a prospect which is neither likely nor, other than for a
small number of hard-line activists, terribly attractive
– or serious reform of existing neoliberal and supranational institutions (which have, by and large, proved
themselves unreformable to any meaningful degree),
any resistance must come from nation states enacting
measures which have the potential to disrupt the status
quo. They might do this in a range of ways. One is
to weaken – where desirable by seceding from – those
supranational institutions which seek to embed the pre-

cepts of globalisation within national economies and legislation. Of course that doesn't of itself guarantee that an elected government won't then fill the space with its own version of domestic neoliberalism – the democratic principle does, after all, rightly compel us to accept the outcome of elections – but it does potentially undermine some of the fundamental pillars propping up the current system.

That is one of the many – but nonetheless a key – reason why the Left should have led the charge for Brexit. Not because secession from the EU was ever an end in itself, but ultimately because it restored democratic control over wide areas of policy to the national parliament, cleared the path for the implementation of a more radical economic programme by a future Labour government, and would have demonstrated that the Left wasn't afraid to strike at globalisation where it was ostensibly strongest. Instead, it ceded the campaign to the Right and paid a crippling price electorally.

A Left government acting in the British national interest and confident about using all the powers available to it – including those repatriated from the EU – could do much in the way of domestic policy to upset the existing global order. It could, for example, defy the neoliberal orthodoxy of the past four-and-a-half decades and take a much more economically interventionist approach by:

- Reversing the privatisation of key utilities and industries and restating the case for public provision as a public good.
- Challenging the assumption that austerity is the correct response to a faltering economy and instead pursuing investment-led growth.
- Striving to end the decades-long overvaluation of sterling which has decimated our manufacturing base

– and destroyed thousands of jobs – by making British goods fundamentally uncompetitive in the international marketplace, thereby contributing to retarded productivity and a perennial trade deficit.

- Instituting full employment, rather than price stability, as the prime goal of economic policy.
- Setting policy unambiguously in the interests of those who live and work in the real economy, where goods are produced and wealth created, and ending the long indulgence of the City and existing asset holders.
- Strengthening trade union rights as a means to securing higher wages and better workplace standards.
- Developing a sound industrial strategy, thus signalling that the government was determined to intervene on behalf of British industry rather than leave matters to the caprices and diktats of the market.
- Implementing an immigration policy which allows for maintenance of control over the labour supply, thereby easing downward pressure on wages and aiding planning around housing, welfare and employment.
- Allowing the Bank of England, under government direction, to create credit to serve the interests of productive industry rather than leave lending as a virtual monopoly in the hands of private banks which direct their funds overwhelmingly towards other priorities (such as housing).
- Committing to retain permanently its own independent currency.
- Restoring the Bank of England to democratic control, so that monetary policy is in the hands of elected politicians rather than unaccountable officials and is designed to give effect to the government's wider economic programme for the real economy rather than submit to the demands of a financial sector overly preoccupied with monetary targets.

- Implementing restrictions on the movement of capital as a means of mitigating the damaging effects to the economy, industries and communities of significant and volatile flows of money in and out of the country, which include the all-too-frequent practice of foreign interests buying up our assets, driving down standards and then repatriating profits. (Capital controls are regarded as taboo by many, and not just free market enthusiasts, but the idea has received endorsement in the past from voices such as the Nobel-prize-winning economist Paul Krugman[3] and even – albeit to a limited extent – the International Monetary Fund.[4] Ultimately, socialists must be prepared to call for controls over the movement of capital in the interests of working people.)

Though many of the above measures were, before the advent of neoliberal economics, considered mainstream across the spectrum of British politics – indeed, much of this agenda underpinned the post-war consensus that lasted through to the 1970s – all would run counter to today's neoliberal orthodoxy, and some of them, particularly if implemented by a major advanced economy such as ours, would represent a blow to the ambitions and hegemony of those who stand behind the global economic system. Indeed, the very concept of a single global market means that any attempt by individual governments to intervene in such a way as to alter the manner in which it operates would, by definition, be seen as a violation.

But before any government, Left or otherwise, could implement such a programme, it would need to have a clear-eyed and unshakeable belief in the value of the nation state and its ability, especially when free from the grip of supranational neoliberal institutions, to resist the demands of international capital, as well as be prepared to use every lever at its disposal to manage the national economy in the interests of its citizens. That would mean abandoning the silly contention that any belief in the nation state is inherently derived from some kind of xenophobia or sense of 'Little Englander' superiority. On the contrary, none of the arguments or ideas set out here preclude a government from striving to play its full role on the international stage and continuing to work in partnership with neighbours and allies on matters of mutual interest, such as trade and security.

Furthermore, a group of nation states acting collaboratively towards these ends has the real potential to both reinvigorate national democracy and refashion the global economic order to bring about a shift in power and influence away from business chiefs, international investors, bankers, technocrats and the super-rich and towards elected governments, national parliaments and ordinary voters. Indeed, any movement desirous of achieving such radical transformation must understand from the outset that, to better resist the inevitable attempts by the upholders of the status quo to isolate and punish any individual nation set on such a path, the highest degree of international co-operation between those of the same mind would be necessary.

Such co-operation would again demonstrate that the spirit of genuine internationalism – in this case, solidarity between independent self-governing nation states and their peoples resolved to run their own affairs – was something very different from the beast of globalisation.

## *Understanding the patriotism of the working classes*

Any political party with such a programme at its heart would be sure to attract significant support from the ranks of the working class and, to a degree, beyond them. The deep anger at the violations, inequities and injustices of the global economy that have led to the growth of populist and patriotic movements across much of the West is, as we have seen, felt across much of the British electorate. Brexit, as I have argued, was not only a verdict on the benefits or otherwise of membership of the EU, but a symptom of a much wider discontent; it can therefore, in that context, be seen as the clearest backlash yet against the predominance of a global order underpinned by neoliberalism. That sentiment isn't going to disappear any time soon.

Among so many ordinary voters there is a strong and unabating desire to be free to elect and remove those who make the laws under which they must live; to have decisions made as close to home as possible and by representatives attuned (in a way that the high priests of the global economy never could be) to the national mood and responsive to national needs; to have their government play a full role in running the economy and to do so unapologetically in the national interest and with minimum interference by outside forces; and to know that if their demands go unmet they are truly able to effect change through the ballot box rather than be told that there is no alternative.

But though it is vital for the Left to rethink its view of the nation state as a first step to confronting neoliberal globalisation, it would be wrong to consider economic imperatives the only justification for a much-needed rediscovery of nationhood. The ideas of many who

155

fall within the second group of globalisers I identified earlier in the chapter – the political and cultural kind – must also be challenged head on. For their insidious attempts to delegitimise any sense of national pride, and to equate such sentiment with xenophobia and racism, have fuelled divisions and antagonisms within British society and bred resentment among millions of patriotic working-class citizens. Indeed, their attitude is in large part responsible for the revival of national consciousness that we have experienced in recent years.

Fundamentally, this group needs to learn what motivates millions of ordinary people into a patriotism that refuses to be extinguished. It is in no sense driven by animosity towards outsiders or by British 'exceptionalism', but is instead rooted in the simple concepts of tradition and belonging – the product of a shared history, culture, language and religion, of social mores that have, in many cases, been passed down from previous generations. These are not things to be ashamed of; they are the common bonds of identity and solidarity – of life itself – upon which all civilised and cohesive societies are built.

In the same way that these common bonds may bind together those rooted in a particular street or village or town or institution, so they may a country. National identity and pride can therefore be seen as the ultimate expression of communitarianism. Yet while many on the modern Left do not bat an eyelid at demonstrations of pride in all those other cases, they will often frown upon any display of pride in a shared national identity. They do not see that a sense of nationhood built around common bonds and a shared identity is simply an extension of the feelings of attachment and solidarity that are generated by these things at a more local level. (Indeed, it is ironic that those responsible for the growth of identity politics – and, in some cases, its most militant purveyors – try so hard to delegitimise the very identity, *national* identity, that matters most to so many.)

That the sentiment of patriotism often seems strongest among the working class should not come as a surprise. For it is usually those who have been dealt the toughest hand in life – whose financial circumstances are more challenging and whose opportunities in the way of travel or further education or career advancement or cultural exploration are more limited – who feel a heavier pull towards home, community and place. The more restricted the life chances, the greater the sense of rootedness and the more value is attached to relationships and belonging. It could be argued, too, that those who are less wealthy and therefore less mobile have a greater incentive to concentrate their efforts on improving the communities and country in which they spend their lives.

The patriotism of many is drawn from a sense of being part of something greater than themselves and, in return, of being accepted as a valued fellow citizen by others who, in most cases, they will never meet but with whom, nonetheless, they hold much in common.

It is through developing the deepest commonality between people in this way – by fostering a shared solidarity and cultural bonds that lead humans to identify with their fellow citizens and demonstrate a willingness to make sacrifices for them – that societies function most effectively. It's why, for example, a person living in Hampshire would be more willing to see his taxes used to fund regeneration projects and employment initiatives in a deprived town in Lancashire than in, say, Bratislava. Not for a moment because that person does not see residents of Bratislava as fellow human beings, but because he doesn't necessarily see them as fellow citizens of a single political and economic community with a shared identity, history, culture, language and so on.

This may in part explain why some citizens are comfortable with giving money to charities (such as Comic Relief) which aim to improve the lives of those overseas, yet become much less amenable to the idea when the government compels them to do so through the tax system (to fund the budget for overseas aid).

It is also why putative superstates such as the EU will, in trying to replicate these sentiments of national solidarity at a supranational level, always meet with resistance. It's why, too, those on the Left who have argued that the EU should be reformed to make it more democratic and progressive are missing the point. Regardless of whatever ideology underpins the EU and how democratic it might be, securing lasting popular support for an institution whose remit runs across such a geographically dispersed and economically and culturally diverse set of actors will always be an uphill task. Millions of citizens consider the nation state to be the upper limit of a single, democratic political and economic community. The further the attempt to go beyond that, the less legitimacy it will enjoy.

There is a certain hypocrisy at play here, too, in that some on the Left who dismiss the nation state as an artificial historical construct into which people were corralled – often against their will and as some kind of imagined community – will simultaneously contend that the EU (whose common bonds and sense of shared citizenship are, insofar as they exist at all, much weaker than anything that can be found in a single nation state) has the capacity to bring citizens of diverse and dispersed nations together and command their loyalties in the name of some greater Europeanism. Nation states have a single demos. By contrast, there exists no EU demos.

Take the Greek financial crisis of the 2010s. The restrictions that come with membership of a single currency, and in particular the straitjacket of a single monetary policy, meant that the Greeks, unable to pull many of the levers available to governments of nations with an independent currency, could do little more than depend upon the charity, in the form of bailouts, of the more dominant players within the eurozone – such as Germany, which at the time was Greece's main creditor. But many taxpayers in Germany, while regarding the Greeks as fellow humans and not wishing them ill, simply did not see them as fellow citizens of a single political and economic community and – against the backdrop of media coverage portraying the Greeks as 'feckless' – were therefore not disposed towards offering the kind of solidarity in the form of the huge financial assistance required (or at least not without the most stringent conditions attached) that they might have been willing to provide if that assistance were being directed towards hard-pressed folk in, say, Bremen. The perception of Germany as a financial oppressor and of Greece as a financial liability led to tensions between the two countries that existed only as a consequence of the attempt to force them into political and monetary union in the first place.

Such tensions could also be seen in the fall-out from the Covid-19 crisis, when EU member states were at loggerheads in trying to reach agreement over the question of whether there should be some degree of collective burden in taking on whatever debt was required to address the devastating economic impact of the pandemic.

So not only is the nation state the best model of democratic government at its upper level yet invented, it is also the largest unit of governance within which sufficient numbers of citizens have shown themselves willing to demonstrate generosity towards others. Go beyond it, and the elasticity of democracy and social solidarity begins to slacken. That is why any move towards closer political and economic union with other nations or institutions, so far as it is desirable at all, should only ever be made at a pace with which the broad mass of the electorate is comfortable.

Some may argue that the experience of devolution in the UK – which has seen citizens of the respective home nations apparently remaining willing to demonstrate openness and generosity to their neighbours – undermines this argument. I don't accept this. The truth is that devolution, while far-reaching, has not ultimately had the effect of persuading citizens of each UK nation to regard the other constituent nations as somehow 'foreign', and most still look upon the union as a single political and economic entity sustained by deeply embedded historical and cultural ties. Those sort of ties may also go some way towards explaining why British citizens were generally relaxed about their government contributing to a huge financial bailout package for Ireland back in 2010.

### A *meaningful citizenship*

For many on the modern Left, the concept of citizenship is meaningless. Their perception of the relationship between the nation state and the individual as being purely functional, and their consequent disregard for sentiments of belonging or identity or the building of social capital within a national framework, leads them to positions which undermine the very fundamentals of democratic participation. So, for example, the Labour

Party voted at its annual conference in 2019 to support an extension of voting rights to all foreign nationals. Just like that. Everyone resident in Britain, irrespective of where they came from or when, would be allowed to choose the next government in a general election.

If it were ever implemented, such a proposal would surely render the holding of citizenship worthless in democratic terms. The vote of someone who has lived and held citizenship in Britain all his life, holds a British passport, is deeply acquainted with the nation and has a considerable interest in its future, might be cancelled out by that of someone who may have been resident for just a few weeks, has no intention of staying long-term and may have (for entirely understandable reasons) little or no affinity for the country in which he found himself. This proposal was illustrative of how parts of the Left had been captured by the philosophy of 'global citizenship', which, in encouraging humans to see themselves as part of a single worldwide political community, meant they felt no specific loyalty to, or affection for, their own immediate community or country.

Some on today's Left – and particularly the far-left – will often recite slogans such as 'Workers of the world unite!' or 'Build unions, not borders!' when challenging the concept of nationhood and borders. They see these things as roadblocks to their brand of international socialism, as obstacles dividing worker from worker. Of course, developing solidarity across national boundaries is an entirely laudable aim and something commensurate with the labour movement's proud tradition of internationalism. But for many who resort to such sloganising, the international class war is everything, and all things must be subordinated to it. This leads them to see workers – both individually and in their relations with others – principally through the prism of their place in the economic structure, and by extension as some kind of off-the-peg battalion in the battle against capitalism. So they will deploy arguments along the lines of 'We have more in common with each other than with the bosses', as though solidarity on the basis of class were the only thing that mattered.

The problem with this approach, however, is that most working-class people do not see themselves in this narrow way, not necessarily because they lack 'class consciousness', but simply because, for them, class is but one of a multitude of things that may inform their worldview or drive their relations with others. These other things – language, culture, custom, tradition, heritage, nationality, religion, interests, hobbies, vocation, and so on – often matter just as much to them, sometimes more so, than class identity, and all of them have the capacity in some way to draw humans together in solidarity, or indeed drive them apart. To expect individuals, then, to set these factors aside when determining their relationships and political opinions, and to insist that class be the primary, or only, concern, is to assume that they attach to the class struggle a level of importance that is usually reserved for only the most politically committed.

Like it or not, a working-class Labour voter may feel he has more in common with an 'owner of capital' on account of the fact that they speak the same language, live in the same town, believe in the same god, drink in the same pub and support the same football team than he does with a fellow working-class person with whom he holds none of those things in common. And the Left needs to be very careful about implying that it is somehow wrong or ignoble for him to feel that way.

For the truth is that social solidarity is arrived at in a number of different and perfectly legitimate ways, and the Left must learn to navigate all of them rather than resort to trite sloganising that suggests it is all about class. It isn't. Relationships and belonging matter, too.

Some of those on the Left in prominent political positions, though privately ill-disposed towards the nation state, understand that there is a game to be played, and that to demonstrate their hostility openly would be to risk paying a big price electorally. So they will talk about their 'patriotism', but often only in the most nebulous or hackneyed terms. They will, for example, wax lyrical about Britain's 'diversity', 'tolerance' and 'cosmopolitanism' – in other words, any concept or policy that can be associated with the modern liberal or progressive agenda. But rarely do they cite anything explicitly rooted in the nation's history. Thus, they will ignore such things as Magna Carta, the pioneering of parliamentary democracy and individual liberty, *habeas corpus*, the English Bill of Rights, the nation's deep roots in Christianity, its illustrious canon of literature and poetry, and so on. This may be because they are ignorant of these things. Or, more likely, that they are embarrassed enough by the nation's history generally that they are wont to stick to the safe ground of the past couple of decades. Anything further back than that strays dangerously close to the territory of conservativism or, heaven forbid, Empire.

This means that those past struggles and campaigns about which the Left should be readily effusive often get less exposure than they deserve – from the Tolpuddle Martyrs and the Chartists, to the New Unionism of the late twentieth century, the defeat of fascism, and suchlike. The reluctance to acknowledge a world before 1968 (or 1997) prevents many on today's Left from recognising even the best and most radical milestones and events in the country's history.

George Orwell summed up the attitude of the English

intelligentsia in his 1941 essay 'England Your England', when he wrote:

> In the general patriotism of the country, they form a sort of island of dissident thought. England is perhaps the only great country whose intellectuals are ashamed of their own nationality. In Left-wing circles, it is always felt that there is something slightly disgraceful in being an Englishman, and that it is a duty to snigger at every English institution, from horseracing to suet puddings.[5]

### England forgotten: a tale of national dispossession

Very little has changed. There exists today the same arrogant elite, convinced they are the trustees of progressive and enlightened values, and called upon to educate the working classes out of their nativist views. And, as in Orwell's time, this mindset is particularly prevalent among the English intelligentsia in their attitude towards England. In fact, the English have perhaps the greatest cause for grievance at the denial of their sense of nationhood. Whereas liberal politicians and commentators will reluctantly (and, in some cases, not so reluctantly) indulge the sentiments of national pride and identity expressed across other nations of the British Isles, any celebration of Englishness – other, it seems, than in a sporting context – is considered taboo.

In particular, some on the modern Left will tolerate displays of patriotic emotion by the Scots, Welsh and Irish on the grounds that these nations carry less of the baggage of history, Empire and racist sentiment with which England is saddled, and, in the case of Ireland, can legitimately claim to have on occasion been actively oppressed by the dominant partner within these islands. Moreover, some among those other nations have less of the tradition of conservatism – or, worse, Toryism – that contaminates their larger neighbour. Their nationalism is therefore seen as being of the more progressive and less reactionary kind.

It is this narrow perception of an England as an oppressor nation whose hands are soaked with the blood of imperialism and reaction that drives the hostility towards it by much of modern liberal thought. It is a very jaundiced viewpoint: after all, most countries and peoples have mixed histories – darker chapters as well as moments of pride. Nobody's hands are completely clean, yet England surely has as much in her past of which to be proud as most other nations.

This hostility has also, paradoxically, served to intensify a growing English nationalist sentiment – albeit a mainly inchoate and uncoordinated one – in recent years. Many English people have twigged that their sense of patriotism and identity is held as unworthy and illegitimate in the minds of the political and cultural elites. Yet, for the most part, it is motivated only by the same simple and benign feeling of attachment as that which drives such emotions among populaces in other nations. It is manifested through not only a respect for the history and traditions of the country, but also the enjoyment derived from such things as support for the national football team, the English countryside, pop music, pubs, humour, and so on.

Most ordinary folk in working-class communities such as Barking and Dagenham would find it bizarre that anyone should ascribe their patriotism to a yearning for Empire or a sense of national superiority. And they would be angered at the notion that it was attributable to some deep-seated racism. Such a caricature does them a grave disservice, and they know it. It's why, for example, they get angry when they are accused of doing the work of the far-right when displaying the flag of St George. These days, apart from a hardcore few, everyone accepts entirely the view that national identity and citizenship should transcend ethnicity. They understand that a civic nationalism built around shared values and which reaches out to all sections of society is infinitely more desirable than any sort of regressive nationalism centred on racial homogeneity.

The sense of national dispossession that has taken root over recent years in these types of communities – England beyond the cities – shows no sign of dissipating. A feeling of disenfranchisement that began to take hold around the turn of the century, with the advent of devolution in Wales and Scotland, solidified into a more general resentment at being 'forgotten' and then the emergence of a new sense of Englishness, with larger numbers of people beginning to identify as English rather than British. There was a clear mood developing among the English: we are sick and tired of being ignored.

In the EU referendum, this mood manifested itself in the clear rejection of the status quo, with over 70 per cent of those who identified most strongly as English voting Leave. (A similar percentage of those who identified the least strongly voted Remain).[6] The writer and campaigner Anthony Barnett has illustrated how much of the Leave vote was driven by a distinct sense of grievance among the English. Comparing the towns of Wigan in northern England and Paisley in Scotland, he explained how they were similar in the sense that both were 'once thriving centres of imperial industry . . . now grappling with impoverishment' and 'social and economic equivalents'. Yet in the referendum, Wigan voted 64 per cent for Leave and Paisley, on an identical turnout, the same percentage for Remain.[7] Barnett concluded that it was the national factor at work.

In 2018, a poll for the Centre for Towns think-tank showed that the towns in which people identified most strongly as English – often places which had undergone fundamental social and economic change – were most inclined to feel that Westminster did not reflect the concerns of their part of the country.[8]

As this sense of English discontent grows, it does so outside of normal political structures and institutions – principally because it has no other choice. Neither the Conservative nor Labour parties, for example, maintain a specifically English section; and there is no major party, assembly or parliament representing solely England. English voters also see the obvious democratic imbalance of having MPs representing constituencies in other nations of the UK vote on laws affecting England while, thanks to devolution, their counterparts representing English constituencies have no corresponding right.

A YouGov survey for the BBC in 2018 highlighted the extent to which English identity had become a feature of people's lives, with 80 per cent of respondents saying they identified strongly as English.[9] This feeling had taken hold particularly in coastal and former industrial towns, with two-thirds of respondents in those places saying they felt a sense of English pride. By contrast, less than half of respondents in the major cities felt the same thing.

Labour has a particular problem with England, having not beaten the Conservatives in the share of the popular vote there since 2001. It is widely accepted that worries among English voters at undue SNP influence over a future Labour government played a crucial role in helping the Tories achieve a majority at the 2015 general election. And of the sixty seats lost by the Labour Party at the 2019 general election, forty-eight were in England. This was, in large part, the vote that the party had always taken for granted, with many of the losses occurring in traditional working-class heartlands – the so-called 'Red Wall' and non-metropolitan seats – where the sense of patriotism and 'being English' was heightened.

A post-election report for the English Labour Network showed that more voters in England were likely to identify as 'more English than British' than the other way round, and that this group was instrumental in delivering victory for the Conservative Party.[10] Among these voters, Labour won just ten votes for every twenty-seven won by the Conservatives.

The authors, who included former cabinet member John Denham, concluded that Labour's failure to promote itself as a patriotic party or to even mention England in any of its political messaging, as well as its lack of any plan to devolve power within England, had alienated voters who emphasised their English identity. And on the contentious issue of immigration – unquestionably a significant factor on the doorstep – they wrote, perceptively:

> These voters have been disconcerted by mass immigration. Their strong sense of identity and community has been disrupted by changes they were not expecting. While some of this reaction is based on racism, for most it is more [a] sense of uncertainty and loss of a stable community. At least some Labour figures and activists have stereotyped anyone who is not actively in favour of large-scale migration as bigoted.

In its disregard for the growing sense of English dispossession, Labour has repeated the catastrophic mistake it made in Scotland – a failure which led to its virtual wipe-out there – of not paying due attention to the politics of national identity. And until it acknowledges this reality, Labour will not even begin to solve the biggest conundrum facing it: how to maintain (or win back) the support of a working class which increasingly asserts the politics of belonging, identity and cultural traditionalism as an antidote to the very cosmopolitan liberalism to which the party has become so ideologically wedded. There is no reason, other than its own misgivings and prejudices, why Labour could not embrace an English patriotism that is in step with the best of the labour movement's radical and democratic traditions – the kind embodied by the likes of Tony Benn and Michael Foot, the Levellers and the Diggers, Orwell, Wat Tyler and Thomas Paine.

More widely, until Labour and the broader Left recognise the truism that the nation state is not only here to stay, but that, more crucially, it has enormous capacity to do good – improving, if its power is properly harnessed, the lives of working-class people by challenging the precepts and dominance of neoliberal globalisation and providing a foundation stone for meaningful democracy, social cohesion and stability – they will have no role in the nation-building and reconciliation which have become so vital in the wake of the recent convulsions that have struck Britain.

Nothing has yet come along to successfully supplant the nation state as the upper limit of popular democracy. A world of free, independent and democratic nation states working together in the interests of peace and prosperity, but resolved to defend their own sovereignty and run their own affairs in the interests of their own electorates, must therefore be the goal. The British Left must get on board.

# 5

# What is to Be Done?

The British Left is in a quagmire and flirting with irrelevance. As a long-time trade unionist and Labour Party member, it pains me to say such a thing, but there is no escaping it.

The 2019 general election wipe-out represented Labour's worst result since 1935. Conservative rule, underpinned by a huge Commons majority, will almost certainly be a feature of our political landscape for the next five years, probably longer. That the Tories, led by an old Etonian, and after having imposed crippling economic austerity for a decade, were able to win so much support in traditional working-class communities – support which ultimately propelled them to victory – was the clearest demonstration of the dramatic degree to which Labour has lost touch with its heartlands.

Many who are sympathetic to the arguments set out in this book will insist that the Labour Party is a busted flush, and that our efforts must be concentrated on building something new. For a variety of reasons, I do not agree. First, for all its many faults, the Labour Party remains the only UK-wide organisation of the Left that is able to command the support – albeit diminishing –

of sufficient numbers of working-class voters to stand even a chance of winning power. Second, the history of attempts to create a new party on the Left is not exactly an illustrious one. Third, for as long as the institutions which act as the official voice of workers – the trade unions – remain affiliated to Labour, we need to organise with and among them. Ultimately, we must operate where the movement operates. And, fourth, the Labour Party has traditionally swung from Right to Left and back again, sometimes when the chances of any shift seemed remote. For example, who would have predicted just a few months before Jeremy Corbyn became leader the seismic change in the party that was about to occur?

Everything that follows, therefore, is predicated on the belief that, notwithstanding the mountain it needs to climb, the Labour Party remains the only show in town when it comes to organisations of the Left that have the potential to secure enough support to form a government and effect political change designed to improve the lives of working people.

Some within Labour have argued that the party should simply accept that the working-class voters who have abandoned it are gone for ever – that it should surrender all efforts to win them back and instead remodel itself as a party exclusively for the young, the metropolitan, the socially liberal, the graduate, the social activist, the public sector worker, and the middle class. But such a strategy would be profoundly wrong, not only because it is doubtful that Labour would ever be able to win power again on that basis, but – a question which is much more pertinent – what on earth is the party for if it is not to serve as a vehicle for the hopes, aspirations and everyday interests of marginalised and voiceless working-class voters of the type for whom it was created in the first place and who these days can be found across neglected post-industrial, small-town and coastal Britain?

Labour must accept, therefore, that there is no route back to power that does not pass through these places and seek to win the hearts, minds and votes of the people living in them. But how to achieve that? Fundamentally, there needs to be a radical shift in ideology, policy and language. Labour must change itself before it can even think about winning power again. This means, first and foremost, doing something that many in the party will find difficult: they must stop hating large sections of the nation's working class. That is not hyperbole: I state as a fact – drawn from personal experience – that many in the party are contemptuous of the values and priorities of working-class people, and often of the individuals themselves. Until that changes, Labour is finished in many working-class communities.

Labour must start to look and sound more like the voters in these communities. It must begin to speak their language. There must be a recalibration of the entire demographic of the party away from an overwhelmingly urban, liberal and middle-class membership, activist base and parliamentary party, and towards something that better reflects ordinary working-class voters in provincial Britain. This is not to say there should be an effort to drive the former from the party. On the contrary, the party has, as I have argued, always played home to its fair share of middle-class liberals and intellectuals and indisputably been the better for that. It would be foolish, therefore, to argue that Labour should not seek to appeal to this cohort of voters and instead focus exclusively on winning the support of the old industrial working class.

But the historical compromise between these two groups that has always been the prerequisite for Labour election successes has, over the past thirty years, become fatally lopsided, meaning that the coalition itself has now broken apart. As the traditional working-class element has seen so much of the ethos and programme of the party shift in the direction of the interests of the liberal middle class, so it has become disillusioned and jumped ship. Any Labour Party aspiring to govern the country needs broad support from both groups; to alienate one of them is, as we have seen, to court electoral disaster.

In the end, all political organisations must remember that, when looking to develop wider layers of support, they should start with their core vote and build outwards. For Labour, this ought to mean anchoring everything it does in the priorities and aspirations of the working class throughout hard-pressed and provincial Britain, and then seeking to appeal to a sufficient layer of those – often less tribal – graduate and professional classes in the cities and elsewhere. But from the time that New Labour took control of the party, this process went into reverse. The party since then has focused disproportionately on appealing to the second half of that combination while hoping that the working class stayed with it. And, for a time, the working class did. Until all trust was severed. And that has left Labour in the terrible predicament of having been abandoned by large parts of its traditional base.

This whole process has left the Labour Party seriously imbalanced. It struggles to see a world beyond the cities. It is especially London-centric, and too often views the rest of the country as though it were merely the outlying districts of the capital. It could not be more wrong. Though it still has its grittier areas, such as Barking and Dagenham, much of London – particularly the modern, diverse, cosmopolitan, trendy, gentrified quarters – is like nowhere else in Britain, and anyone who sees the entire nation through the lens of the metropolis will inevitably end up with a distorted picture.

The party today is too much Hampstead and not enough Hartlepool. The pendulum needs to shift decisively back the other way. In the way that New Labour calculated in the 1990s that it needed to appeal to greater numbers of the middle class if it was to win power, now it is the working class to whom it must reach out, and it is the middle class, liberal left, young, graduate, metropolitan element of the party which is called upon to make the compromise.

## Looking and sounding like Labour again

Working-class representation has been slowly sucked out of the Labour Party. With less than a quarter of its membership falling into the C2DE social grade, and only a third living in its old heartlands in the northern half of England,[1] there needs to be a concerted effort to tackle the existing unevenness.

Labour must strive as much – arguably, more – to increase working-class representation inside its ranks as it traditionally has that of other under-represented groups. It is, of course, something of a 'chicken and egg' situation: ordinary working-class voters of the type that have been alienated are unlikely to be drawn into the party while its demographic and policy agenda remain unreflective of them and their values, and those things are unlikely to alter in any real sense until there is greater influence from this group. So there are no easy answers. But a start would be to at least understand what needs to be done and to launch major initiatives designed to recruit more working-class members.

Such a drive should aim to appeal to the working class in all its shades and complexities, and offer a home to those who might otherwise feel instinctively Labour but have little truck with its dominant liberal ideology and believe that their small 'c' conservative values are unwelcome in the party. How gratifying it would be, for example, to draw into the labour movement the disadvantaged white voter from Mansfield and bring him together with the Polish Catholic from London, the patriotic Sikh from Slough, the Muslim living in a former northern mill town, and the self-employed 'Essex man' – the types of groups that attach a high value to the concepts of family and place – on the basis of working-class politics and interests.

Those across the labour movement – the clutch of MPs, trade unionists, councillors and members, as well as groups such as Blue Labour, the English Labour Network and Labour Future – who have demonstrated an understanding of the alienation of the working class and what it might take to remedy matters, must work collaboratively in pursuit of this aim while doing whatever they can to influence policy. And they should do so with the confidence of knowing that while they may for the moment be a marginalised voice inside the movement, they have huge political capital through having been proved right, and can be sure that their arguments resonate loudly with swathes of voters who were once proudly Labour and would be so again if those arguments held sway in the party.

These individuals and groups will, by intervening and organising at all levels of the movement – in local Labour parties, affiliated societies and trade unions – help to shift the direction of travel. The grassroots Corbynite group Momentum, for all its many shortcomings, showed how, through slick and well-organised campaigning, it is possible to effect swift and radical change in a movement that may appear leaden and ideologically static.

Trade unions themselves – so often in the past a route into labour movement politics for ordinary workers – can do their bit by emerging from their metropolitan and public sector redoubts and organising more effectively across private industry and provincial Britain.

A more overtly working-class labour movement would also be more effective at challenging the national class divide, which, even in this era of so-called 'meritocracy', sees so few individuals from working-class backgrounds break through the glass ceiling, and still ringfences most of the plum jobs across politics, the media, the law, public services and business for those born into wealth and privilege. This form of social apartheid, which so tragically stunts opportunity and wastes genuine working-class talent, continues to shame our country.

Electorally, the Labour Party must understand that it is likely to win power again only if it is able to exploit that sweet spot on the political spectrum where millions of working-class (and, indeed, many middle-class) voters can be found. These voters support a more egalitarian economy, such as through redistribution of wealth, the richest paying a higher share of tax, tackling boardroom excesses and regional inequalities, reducing the gap between rich and poor, increasing the minimum wage and so on. But as well as wanting economic security, they also long for a greater degree of cultural security. They desire a more communitarian approach to social policy. They want politicians to respect their way of life and sense of place. They want them to start speaking the language of home, place, family, relationships, work and nation – concrete things that really matter to them – instead of hammering on about modish concepts such as 'diversity', 'inclusivity' and 'equality'. They do not see themselves, or their families and communities, as commodities to be exploited or uprooted in the name of an unrestrained global capitalism that demonstrates no respect for the human desire to belong nor any recognition of the value of social solidarity. They don't believe that everything must be subordinated to the pursuit of economic growth or profit. They may have some socially conservative views and object to being treated as museum pieces in their own country. And when they speak through the ballot box, as they did with Brexit, they expect their wishes to be implemented.

Most of these voters have similar expectations in how their country should be run and about the proper role of government. They don't demand miracles, and they know government has its limitations. But they wish for an opportunity to secure dignified work and decent wages; for their children to have a fair chance of getting on the housing ladder; for public services that do what they are supposed to do; for the streets to be safe; to have enough spare cash in their pocket to enjoy regular leisure time and an annual holiday; to live in a nation characterised by steady and stable families and communities, and of which all citizens feel proud to be a part. These voters don't object to people getting on in life; they just ask for the same chances. It really isn't complicated.

Whether or not they truly believe in it, the Tories under Boris Johnson at least demonstrate an understanding of all this. They have appealed to the millions throughout Britain who, on the one hand, were ingrained with these values and priorities and, on the other, rejected any notion that their lives should be dominated by a rapacious market, an overbearing state, or the precepts of cosmopolitan liberalism, all of which, in various ways, have come to symbolise so much of the thinking of our ruling elites. The message to these communities from the Tories – that they understood what was important to them and were willing to use the protective state to improve their lives – resonated loudly and allowed the Conservative Party to reap the dividends at the 2019 election. Until this penny drops with Labour, it will remain in opposition.

### A radical economic policy

We should, though, give credit where it is due. Labour under Jeremy Corbyn took broadly the right approach economically by shifting the party's position from something resembling 'austerity-lite' towards a more radical, egalitarian and anti-austerity policy. This programme – perhaps not surprisingly after several years of economic privation – enjoyed popularity throughout much of the country.

Though 'Corbynomics', as it became known, was portrayed by its critics as redolent of rigid Soviet-style command economies, much of it was in fact built around the kind of mixed-economy, Keynesian interventionist philosophy that has become the stock in trade of Scandinavian economies and that underpinned the economic consensus in Britain that lasted for three decades from the end of the Second World War, only to eventually be supplanted by what we now call neoliberalism.

There is nothing particularly revolutionary about this approach, and there is no need for Labour to step back from it. Voters across all classes and backgrounds in Britain want a fairer economic system. There is a recognition – particularly in light of the global financial crash – that the market is not infallible, that market out-comes are not always better, and that the market should not be allowed to reign supreme over our lives.

None of this is to say that the Left should indulge the most militant voices among its ranks by adopting an anti-market position. On the contrary, it must be acknowledged that markets are not only essential to the functioning of a free and democratic society, but are often the best mechanism by which to allocate scarce resources, reward effort, stimulate dynamism and inno-vation, and raise living standards. A flourishing private sector must therefore be an objective of any party seek-ing to govern from the Left.

There is a growing acceptance, though, that in the relationship between government and market the former must play the role of master and not servant, and that where the market falls short, government must intervene to put things right.

In particular, Labour must stick resolutely to its anti-austerity line. This is not only the correct approach in principle – austerity, after all, impacts most severely on the poorest and most disadvantaged – but it makes sound economic sense, too. In fact, one of the most depressing aspects of the fall-out from the global finan-cial crisis was the reaction of politicians who resorted to the failed nostrums of the past in their attempts to kickstart the economy. In applying austerity measures, these politicians – in the form of the governing Tories and Liberal Democrats in Britain – ignored the lesson from as long ago as the 1930s that retrenchment, in sucking activity from the economy and ultimately chok-ing off recovery, is the worst possible response to an economic crisis, and that the most propitious route to restoring sustainable growth is through encouraging activity by way of investment (which in turn allows for

179

the reduction of any deficit more speedily through max-
imised tax revenues).

The decade of austerity we have experienced in Britain
in the wake of the global financial crisis, as well as being
literally counter-productive, has caused considerable
suffering to working-class communities and weakened
the public services upon which they rely. Though the
worst of it may now be behind us, these questions are,
in the wake of the colossal and unprecedented public
expenditure directed towards overcoming the Covid-
19 pandemic, bound to confront us again, and perhaps
for some years to come, with the likelihood that the
Conservative government will be tempted to employ
similar remedies again as a response to any economic
meltdown.

Moving forwards, then, Labour must continue to
develop a radical broader economic doctrine. The aim
must be to create the type of bold but sound policy
platform – built around reindustrialisation, full employment, investment, strong public services, secure and
sustainable jobs, and reducing income and wealth
inequality – that would win support from the East End
of Glasgow to Middle England, appealing to working-
class and middle-class voters alike – the same coalition
that is the key to winning elections.

Labour must challenge unremittingly the neoliberal
orthodoxy that places undue faith in market outcomes
and the wisdom of business chiefs and bankers – and
by extension sees the proper role of government as little
more than that of a bit-part actor. The party must argue
for an alternative that establishes government as a key
player in the economic life of the nation, prepared to
assume full control over macroeconomic policy and use
all the tools at its disposal – fiscal as well as monetary
– to achieve its desired outcomes. This would mean, by

definition, the restoration of democratic control over the Bank of England.

An overarching philosophy of this kind would – especially when set alongside the freedom that comes with being outside the European Union – create the space for a programme to bring about a fundamental reordering of economic priorities designed to elevate the interests of the real economy over the priorities of the financial markets. A cue might even be taken from Winston Churchill, who in 1952 said he would rather see 'finance less proud and industry more content'.

Full employment should be instituted as the prime goal of economic policy, not only because the denial of the opportunity to work and contribute to society to someone who wishes to do so is a personal tragedy for the individual and his family, nor that society also loses out through the wasting of talent and the cost of increased benefit payments and lost tax revenues, but because nothing would more convincingly send the message that the days of government believing that monetary targets were all that mattered when determining economic success were at an end.

It is true that workers operate today in all sorts of new and different ways. Millions are employed as agency workers or in transient and insecure jobs – the 'precariat' as they have become known – many of them in the gig economy or on zero-hours contracts. And with the emergence of new industries such as green energy, and ongoing advances in technology heralding an era of automation and artificial intelligence, there will be further – and rapid – revolutions in the world of work. The labour movement must anticipate these changes and promote an industrial strategy designed to harness them to the benefit of workers, ensuring particularly that they don't exacerbate

181

existing inequalities or diminish workplace standards and protections.

However, any industrial strategy must not be so pre-occupied with the future that it has a blind spot on established industries and sectors. It must, for example, place the revitalisation of our manufacturing sector at its heart. The decline of British manufacturing – in 1980 it accounted for almost 30 per cent of GDP; now it is less than 10 per cent[2] – and, with it, the obliteration of entire industries and millions of steady blue-collar jobs and apprenticeships, underlies many of our wider economic woes, including our perennial trade deficit.

Some say that in a world in which low-cost competitors abound, reviving our manufacturing base is a pipe dream. Yet the sheer scale of the decline in the UK is unique among major economies (the likes of Germany and Japan, for example, have managed to maintain far more successful manufacturing sectors). One of the principal reasons for the evisceration of manufacturing in Britain – yet one so rarely talked about in politics – is our chronic lack of competitiveness, caused in large part by an overvalued currency. A high pound – again the consequence of a desire by governments over time and of all stripes to indulge the wishes of finance capital and existing asset holders over the interests of those who live and work in the real economy – has had the effect of pricing British goods out of the international marketplace, sucking in imports, and destroying firms and jobs. This has, in turn, disincentivised investment and retarded productivity and growth.

A future Labour government committed to reindustrialisation should, therefore, seek to bring about a more competitive currency and be willing to face down vested interests advancing the usual objections that are rarely borne out by the evidence. For example, critics would argue that such a policy would inevitably result in a rise in inflation. Yet, as the economist and businessman John Mills documented after studying the after-effects of currency devaluations around the world, inflation rarely rises by more than it was rising anyway – or even at all – when the value of a currency falls (usually because a range of disinflationary economic factors take effect).[3]

With the tendency of capitalism, particularly in its more cut-throat neoliberal form, to commodify humanity and nature, and to concentrate wealth and power in ever-fewer hands, the Left must stick to the old tried and tested methods of seeking to constrain it by way of organising through the democratic institutions of the labour movement and beyond.

Trade unions, of course, have traditionally played a crucial role in that objective, which is why attempts to neuter them by way of restrictive legislation should always be opposed. But then so have relational institutions such as credit unions, friendly societies, co-operatives, faith groups, and various other voluntary or campaigning groups. Some of these now barely exist at all or are, at best, disempowered. Yet these 'little platoons' – cornerstones of the early Labour tradition – are weapons in any struggle to resist the domination of capital and to fill that critical space between market and state that is the lifeblood of civil society. That's why the Left should breathe new life into them and encourage their activities wherever possible.

In the context of the catastrophic failure of the commercial banking system, there is surely also now a place – as part of wider industrial and economic policy aimed at rebalancing the economy and promoting growth – for a new network of local and specialist banks supporting enterprises through investment finance and with an interest in ensuring the economic success of the part of the country or sector they serve.

Against the background of the failings of privatisation – manifested variously through higher costs, inferior services and large taxpayer subsidies – there is a compelling case to return some key industries, such as energy, water, Royal Mail and the railways, to public ownership. Polling evidence shows that taking these industries into public ownership would be popular among voters: the Left should therefore be bold about campaigning for it. But it would be important, too, to consider different forms of public ownership and to avoid imposing a monolithic and technocratic state machine over these industries. Embedding the voices of stakeholders – such as workers, users, and local residents – in governance structures would be vital. In particular, any move to a publicly owned and better-integrated rail network must be accompanied by a plan to improve connectivity to Britain's forgotten and declining coastal towns.

With a view to giving workers a greater stake in private industry and a stronger voice in how their enterprises are run, Labour should consider more seriously initiatives such as 'workers on boards' and employee share ownership schemes. The first, common throughout parts of Europe, would help to challenge existing power structures, improve corporate governance and widen industrial democracy. The second, though often viewed with suspicion in left-wing circles, is in fact an idea with a long socialist history, and one that has been supported in various forms by the likes of Bernie Sanders and Jeremy Corbyn. Ultimately, there is no reason why socialists should not support this extension to social ownership, which would have the effect of diffusing power and wealth in industry and commerce, and allow workers to enjoy a share of the profits their labour helps to create.

## The importance of vocation

The Left should ensure that, as an antidote to the capitalist impulse to commodify the labour force, the concept of 'the dignity of labour' – essentially that work brings dignity, and all work, whether it be done by hand or brain, and workers, are worthy of equal respect – is the bedrock upon which all of its thinking and interventions around the economy and the world of work are established. This, in turn, should lead it to reassert the importance of vocational skills and education.

The fashion for viewing some jobs as dirty or menial or undertaken only by the less bright is at the root of many of the problems we face in industry and society. It was presumably this type of thinking that led the Tony Blair government to dream up a crackpot plan to push 50 percent – a seemingly arbitrary figure – of young adults through higher education. The consequences of this policy can be seen today in the number of young adults who spend years working hard at university only to leave with degrees which prove to be of little value and then end up doing jobs they would most likely have secured anyway. They can also be seen in the crippling lack of British workers with vocational qualifications and skills – plumbers, builders, electricians and suchlike – which is, in part, the reason we have become so reliant on cheap imported labour.

Serious consideration must be given to converting several of our universities to vocational colleges, the better to address the skills gap, improve productivity and reassert the value of skilled work. In this vein, renewing our country's proud – but now practically moribund – tradition of apprenticeships should also be a priority.

A recognition of the value and dignity of work should lead us to be wary of ideas such as Universal Basic Income (UBI) as proposed solutions for the effects of a rapidly altering labour market. UBI – though undoubtedly well-meaning – would have the effect of disempowering workers, undermining collective organisation, social solidarity and the principle of reciprocity, and ultimately handing to the state obligations that ought rightfully to lie with employers. In the end, workers need jobs, opportunity and agency, not promises of pocket money.

Instead, Labour should adopt policies such as a 'jobs guarantee' that, as well as showing value for work and offering greater electoral appeal, would demonstrate the party's willingness to intervene in the economy to the purpose of achieving macroeconomic goals – in this case, full employment – that go beyond mere monetary targets.

### Promoting social stability and solidarity

If there's one thing that the past decade has taught us, however, it's that having the right economic programme is not enough. The general elections of 2017 and 2019 in particular demonstrated how the working class will not be won over solely by pledges of a fairer economy and increased prosperity. Economic radicalism must ultimately be matched to a social agenda that also appeals.

This is where Labour and the wider Left have come unstuck. So far as they have attempted to court voters in working-class communities, it is largely by promising to put more pounds in their pocket and by refashioning the economy in their favour. This is attractive only to a point. For if fine words about economic justice are not accompanied by a plan that takes account of these voters' wider social aspirations, and speaks to their vision of the type of society in which they wish to live, it is unlikely these days – as we have seen – to command mass support.

Labour and the Left must therefore begin to speak candidly about those social and cultural topics – what might be called the 'doorstep' issues – that voters wish to talk about but which cause many of their activists to break out in a sweat whenever they are raised in conversation. The fringe issues need to take their rightful position in the order of priorities. There is a place for campaigning over human rights, climate change, trans rights, Palestine, migrants' rights, and so on; but any party or movement that constantly places these causes front and centre cannot aspire to be a serious electoral force.

The Left must learn to stop talking about only the issues it wishes to talk about and start engaging with voters over topics *they* wish to talk about – things they see as relevant to their daily lives. Economic security, yes, but also family, work, community, immigration, national identity, law and order, the welfare system – matters usually dismissed as the preserve of the Right and on which, for some peculiar reason, anything but the most liberal interpretation cannot be considered as consistent with the socialist tradition.

This doesn't mean, of course, that the Left should adopt some kind of tubthumping reactionary line on these issues. It would, for example, plainly be unconscionable for anyone on the Left to resort to anything like a 'send them all back' approach on immigration or to pepper its discourse around welfare with talk of 'spongers', and suchlike. But it needs to be understood that there are serious, nuanced arguments on many of these issues which may easily be articulated by someone who considers himself to be of the Left, which are entirely in keeping with the Labour tradition, and which cannot be casually dismissed as appealing to the lowest common denominator.

For example, on the question of family, there is an overwhelming body of evidence to show that children who are raised with two parents in a stable family unit have better outcomes than those who aren't. It is within the family structure that humans first learn about rules, love, sacrifice, solidarity, respect, compassion, loyalty and obligation. It is there, too, that the common good is elevated over self-interest, a place where one is literally one's brother's keeper. And it is for these reasons that some on the Left have, in the past at least, seen the family unit as socialism in action.

Yet there is a view widespread on today's Left that any belief at all in the virtue of family is intrinsically 'right-wing', and that to promote the traditional family unit in which both parents feature is somehow to 'stigmatise' those who don't live according to this arrangement. 'Families come in all shapes and sizes' is the well-worn refrain deployed to deflect any serious debate around the issue. But this approach must be tackled head on, for it is contributing to industrial-scale suffering and adversity that disproportionately affects the very people whose interests the Left claims to represent.

Research carried out for the Centre for Social Justice (CSJ), for example, shows the UK to have one of the highest percentages of lone parents in Europe.[4] Half of all children will not grow up with both parents, and over a million have no meaningful contact with their fathers. Critically, the consequences of family breakdown for these children are often dire, with an increased chance of their turning to drugs or alcohol, suffering from depression, performing poorly at school, developing behavioural problems and living in poverty in the future. The whole of society pays when families break up.

What on earth is socialist about turning a blind eye to all this? Why should anyone on the Left not wish to avert such outcomes for young people? What is so 'right-wing' about arguing that the life chances of children are improved through having strong family structures around them, and that a family unit in which both parents are present and play an active role in bringing up their young is the most favourable model?

It goes without saying that many single parents are not responsible for the predicament in which they find themselves and do a superb job in raising their children. And society should, of course, give those parents all reasonable support in that effort. But that should not prevent us from saying unequivocally that children's interests are best served through being raised in a home with both parents, and that, while no society should seek to compel couples to stay together, our culture, laws, and tax and benefits system should at least be designed to facilitate this outcome for the maximum number possible.

These are not fringe views. On the contrary, they are common currency across our land. The CSJ study, for example, showed that 72 per cent of adults believe that family breakdown is a serious problem, 64 per cent consider fatherlessness in the same way, and 69 per cent consider it important that children grow up living with both parents.

For the older generation, too, the collapse of family life has brought misery, with the epidemic of divorce and separation leading to increasing levels of estrangement between parents and their offspring and an eventual, painful loneliness for many as they enter their twilight years. According to the CSJ, around a quarter of a million people aged over seventy-five now spend Christmas day alone.

Moreover, a side effect of soaring family breakdown, though one rarely talked about, is the increased pressure on an already tight housing market which, in turn, makes the challenge for young families struggling to get a foot on the ladder even tougher.

For all these reasons, the Left should have no compunction in adopting an explicitly pro-family stance and making it the foundation stone of social policy, knowing that in doing so it promotes an institution that stands in the best traditions of solidarity and collectivism, gives youngsters the most propitious start in life, and reduces the likelihood of people growing old in isolation. To this end, it should go beyond settling only for pro-family tax breaks and workplace rights, and be innovative in its design of policy. In Singapore, for example, citizens are given significant grants for choosing to live near to their parents, the better to sustain family support networks. That's the type of thinking we need.

While, of course, no society should prohibit an individual who wishes to work from doing so – and it goes without saying that greater independence and equality for women has been a good thing – the Left might wish to think about the impact on family life of an economic system that, in many cases, compels both parents to go out to work as a matter of financial necessity, and of a culture that views a stay-at-home parent as a personal failure. The evidence showing that working-class families are more likely than middle-class ones to experience fracture is arguably explained – in part, at least – by the fact that it is in poorer families that the pressure for both parents to work is greatest.[5] Any movement that genuinely had the interests of both children and the wider working class at heart would surely wish to put up some resistance to these things.

On immigration, the Left must renounce support for excessively liberal systems. Free-movement-style policies were, as I mentioned earlier, traditionally championed only by those on the fringes of the movement – those for whom it was always only ever about the 'class war' – with the mainstream recognising that control of the labour supply was an important weapon in the armoury of any government serious about defending wages and maintaining its ability to plan effectively around employment, welfare, housing, and so on. But today that position has reversed completely: a commitment to open borders is an article of faith throughout much of the movement, and control over immigration a minority position.

This shift has contributed significantly to the collapse in support for the Labour Party and its estrangement – along with that of the wider labour movement – from working-class voters. The Left needs to understand that there is no incompatibility between, on the one hand, supporting immigration and arguing that it enriches our country while, on the other hand, believing that numbers must be properly regulated so as to maintain faith in the system.

The Brexit vote threw into sharp relief the strength of opposition among the working class to open borders. That opposition was not born out of xenophobia or racism, nor, as many on the Left are wont to claim, was it merely a proxy for other grievances. It was their considered judgement after witnessing the impact of such a policy on their lives, communities and country. The policy of open borders has commodified humanity in the interests of capital, caused downward pressure on the wages of many workers, undermined social solidarity and cohesion, and ultimately made toxic the entire debate about immigration in our country.

It needn't have been this way. But our membership of the European Union, coupled with governments of all persuasions taking an intensely relaxed approach to immigration (despite the protests by some of them to the contrary), meant that people's concerns were never properly addressed and the issue became a running sore in our society. In a more sane world, it ought to have been possible to design a sensible, bespoke immigration policy that accommodated the demands of the public while staying true to the values of tolerance and compassion.

Now, as the nation forges a future outside the EU, the Left cannot avoid the debate about future immigration policy. Sticking to the same old arguments and tactics would be senseless. Hearts and minds will be won back only through a dramatic shift in attitude and language. For a start, the sloganising and patronising must stop. The broad mass of the working class will not be won round to a position of support for open borders by being enjoined to stop 'scapegoating immigrants' or having the supposed benefits of such a policy explained to them a little more forcefully. They oppose open borders because they oppose open borders. And the Left – rather than acting like some arrogant tourist who, when confronted by a native shop assistant who doesn't speak his language, thinks the answer is simply to shout a bit louder – had better star͏ ͏ ing it.

͏ ͏ ͏ ͏ttempt here to set out a detailed and pre-
͏ ͏ ͏ ͏igration policy that would better appeal
͏ ͏ ͏ ͏ass voters. Any debate seeking to arrive at

such a policy would inevitably be complex and multi-faceted. However, any future policy on immigration must be underpinned by some essential features which would likely command broad support.

On the question of refugees, for example, the UK should always be willing to take its fair share of those who can demonstrate that they were compelled to leave their own countries as a consequence of persecution or a threat to their life. What other approach could a humane society possibly take?

On economic immigration, however, there must be a points-based system – subject to regular tweaking – and an annual cap on numbers. Any points-based system should focus on important criteria such as skills, qualifications, proficiency in speaking English, gaps in the labour market, and so on. It is vital, however, that future immigration protocols guard against reliance by employers on regular supplies of cheap imported labour at the expense of paying higher wages to native workers or investing in better training or new technologies.

We have seen the economic and social pressures that come to bear when the yearly net immigration figure tops six figures, so something in the tens of thousands should be the aim, with a limit too on gross immigration. These caps must be rigidly enforced, with no excuses for failure entertained. There should be an understanding that quality-of-life factors must come before any crude considerations about GDP.

It isn't all about numbers, though. Efforts should be made to ensure new arrivals – be they refugees or economic migrants – are, so far as is practical, dispersed as widely as possible throughout the country, the better to promote assimilation and cohesion, as well as preventing sudden and intense pressure on already hard-pressed working-class communities. More regular censuses may be necessary to allow governments to better monitor trends.

On national identity, the Left must start recognising that the instinctive patriotism of millions of working-class people is not driven by xenophobia or a sense of national superiority, but is instead a simple statement of affinity for their own country, motivated by a sense of shared history, tradition, custom and social mores. It must acknowledge, too, the nation state as the upper limit of popular democracy and refrain from initiating any campaign to drag the UK back into the EU. Until the British Left can shake off the growing perception of itself as unpatriotic or, worse, privately ashamed of its own country, it will struggle to recover the support it has lost in working-class communities.

This is not an argument for the Left to embrace some kind of blind jingoistic sentiment. We don't need to force children to salute the flag and sing the national anthem in school assemblies. But it is an appeal for the Left to understand the quiet, often understated, patriotism of millions of ordinary working-class voters.

The People's History Museum in Manchester holds within its collection the earliest trade union banner, made for the Tin Plate Workers' Society in 1821. Emblazoned in one corner of the banner is the Union Flag – a nod to the patriotism of the Society's members. There was never any contradiction between socialist politics and affection for country, and today's Left needs to rediscover those roots.

Nation-building – developing common bonds and fostering a sentiment of shared citizenship and belonging across all sections of society – should be at the heart of politics across the labour movement from now on. The destructive creeds of identity politics and state-sponsored ⁻lticulturalism, which, in actively promoting separateness and division, are wholly inimical to this objective, must be ditched.

In particular, the sense of national dispossession and disenfranchisement felt by the English must be addressed. One way of doing this would be to grant them direct political representation through the creation of a parliament for England to take its place inside a federal United Kingdom.

On law and order, the Left must begin to understand that working-class voters are increasingly frustrated at a police service and justice system that fail to do what they are supposed to do in protecting them from crime and punishing wrongdoers swiftly and effectively. They see repeat offenders consistently evade real justice and those who have committed serious crimes returned to our streets too quickly. Crimes – such as burglary – which cause deep personal distress to many, have appalling conviction rates and are sometimes not even properly investigated. They know that court sentences are largely a sham; they suspect that crime figures are manipulated (as indeed they are); and they see that the police have all but disappeared from their streets and been redeployed as an army of social workers preoccupied with proving their woke credentials.

Many working-class communities are blighted by anti-social behaviour and other general day-to-day lawlessness. Indeed, the working class is, more than any other section of society, most likely to be the victim of crime. The propensity of authorities to treat criminals themselves as victims therefore breeds resentment in those who play by the rules and know right from wrong. The modern Left naturally takes a high-minded sociological approach to these issues, arguing, for example, that the closure of youth services or the abolition of the education maintenance allowance is to blame for youngsters turning to drug-dealing or vandalism. There is, it seems, always an underlying reason for wrongdoing.

It is undoubtedly important to ensure that provision is in place to keep young people occupied and help turn them into useful members of society. But, contrary to the belief of many on the Left, free will still exists, and we should not seek constantly to explain away bad behaviour by recourse to arguments about a lack of opportunity and deprivation. (We might also remember that our country had lower levels of crime during periods, such as the 1930s, when the problems of deprivation and lack of opportunity were far more acute.)

Likewise, on welfare, most working-class people consider the issue through the prism of what is right and just. They support a welfare system that is fair and generous. However, they know they must pay for it, so they believe the system should be robustly managed, and help should go to those in genuine need. They want it to be a safety net and not a comfort blanket. Again, they simply expect their fellow citizens to play by the rules.

Many also believe that a welfare system should be built around the principles of reciprocity and mutual obligation – something for something – over unconditional entitlement. Such an approach, after all, goes to the heart of what social solidarity is about. That is why Labour should do what it has for years been threatening to do and revive the contributory principle that was a key plank of the 1942 Beveridge report. And a system of this kind should take account of social as well as financial contributions, such as by recognising the efforts of those who have looked after parents or children, or given of themselves in some other way to enhance the life of their community.

as they have with so many other 'sensinany on the Left have tried to squash any

serious debate about welfare reform, rejecting any grievances over abuse of the system by denying it happens
or resorting to trite arguments such as: 'Yes, but what
about white-collar crime.'

But maintaining faith in any welfare system is para-
mount. Voters want to see a system that is relational
rather than transactional, one that encourages people
to work rather than not, families to stay together rather
than fragment, and self-reliance over dependency. Any
welfare system that is cold, bureaucratic and devoid of
any moral framework risks forfeiting that faith. And
one that ingrains what former Labour MP Frank Field
described as 'a form of permanent serfdom' does not
ultimately serve the interests of those it is designed to
help.

## Climbing the mountain

All these arguments around family, immigration,
national identity, crime and welfare will, of course, be
dismissed as terribly 'reactionary' and 'uncivilised', and
will jar with the sensibilities of enlightened progressives. But they are the opinions of millions of decent
working-class people up and down our country, including many current and former Labour voters, and they
are fundamentally right. For as long as the Left refuses
to understand why so many working-class people think
the way they do on these issues, or to dismiss the issues
themselves as 'right-wing', it will be more and more out
of step with them and their priorities.

There can be no rapprochement between the working class and the Left while the latter continues to view
the former with scorn and dismiss its grievances and
anxieties. Instead of playing the role of a healing force

in society and overcoming divisions, today's Left seems intent on entrenching them.

The modern Left has proved itself atrocious at reconciling estranged interests or espousing the politics of One Nation. It has instead immersed itself variously in divisive identity politics, cultural elitism, hyper-liberalism and class warfare. Its worldview today is rooted in the politics of both the 1960s radical liberal and the hard-line revolutionary – a movement offering a rather unappealing blend of Lennon and Lenin. It has, in a nutshell, been losing a culture war that occasionally it didn't even realise it was fighting.

Though its more dogmatic activists might take comfort in knowing they are maintaining their ideological purism, facing down the forces of reaction and staying true to 'the struggle', the reality these days is that a movement in their image has only a limited appeal in Britain. In the end, any movement that purports to speak for the working class yet rejects the working-class values of so many – and, worse, holds them in contempt – is asking for trouble.

The question for the Labour Party, which is now infected from top to bottom with this type of politics, is whether it is serious enough about winning power again to acknowledge the dramatic ideological shifts it will need to undergo to reconnect with those working-class voters, such as my old friends and neighbours in Barking and Dagenham, who no longer see the party as their natural home.

The signs are not good. Since the calamitous 2019 general election, many in the party have refused to reflect, kidding themselves that the loss was chiefly the result of either Brexit or a hostile media, and that a 'one more heave' strategy will deliver victory next time round. These people are too certain that the rightness of their beliefs will eventually become apparent to the broad mass of the electorate to entertain any thought of changing strategy. So there must be no compromise with the voters before that day comes.

Yet Britain needs, as much as ever, a strong labour movement to defend the working class from the increasingly predatory demands of an unmediated capitalism, to ensure they enjoy a greater share in the nation's wealth, to defend their jobs and wages and pensions, to build the homes they need to raise their families, to protect the NHS and other public services, and to do all the things it has traditionally done to advance the interests of those whom it was created to represent. A failure, therefore, to get its act together so that it may fulfil this historic role once again would be the greatest betrayal.

The Left desperately needs a new vision – one anchored in the traditions of the labour movement but still fit to serve the needs of working-class people today. A vision that is unremittingly post-liberal and speaks to the human instinct for solidarity and belonging; and one that strives for economic justice but, in doing so, pursues a plan for wider society that elevates the relational over the transactional, the local over the global, and the communitarian over the cosmopolitan.

A vision that understands that most working-class people are social and parochial beings for whom family, place, work, their association with their fellow humans and participation in community life – and the love and relationships that derive from these things – have a very deep and abiding meaning; and one that recognises, too, that these people often place a high value on social solidarity and understand that it is their entry point into society.

A vision that champions a popular, democratic resistance to capitalism and its tendency to commodify humanity and nature, and does so by promoting the self-organisation of the working class through the institutions of the labour movement and beyond. One that also appreciates the fundamental importance of civic community and public service.

A vision that defends freedom of speech and thought as the very essence of democracy and liberty and, while respecting differences, seeks through fostering the deepest social bonds and shared values to overcome, rather than accentuate, them.

Such a vision must recognise that neither the unrestrained market nor the overmighty, impersonal state are ultimately a substitute for human solidarity and mutual self-help – for the very concept of society itself – and the happiness and benefits they bring. It must also abandon notions of class war and seek instead to build a politics of the common good by bringing together conflicting interests.

The Left must ensure that its new vision is internationalist but also deeply patriotic, and sees the nation as a home and not a shop. It must recognise that the best of the labour movement is both radical and conservative, and that the movement can forge a future without surrendering one in favour of the other.

Crucially, any new vision must reject the liberal consensus – economic and social – that has promoted individualism over the common interest and atomised swathes of our country. It must also appreciate the value of our national and cultural inheritance and how it nourishes and sustains us as human beings.

Post-industrial, small-town and coastal communities in Britain have been ignored for too long by an arrogant cultural and liberal elite which has seen those who inhabit these places and their patriotic and traditional values as backward, benighted and a drag on the nation's inexorable journey to the sunlit uplands of cosmopolitan liberalism.

The reckoning was a long time coming but, when it came, it came with a roar. The UK is out of the EU, the Red Wall has crumbled, and the labour movement stands marginalised from the mainstream of society.

We have learned that any drive to create an 'open', 'diverse' and 'progressive' nation will alienate a large part of the populace if it is forced upon them too rapidly, violates their sense of order and belonging, and comes at the expense of social solidarity and stability.

The British working class has found its voice. Politics in our country is realigning at speed as the old tribalisms crumble. The Left, if it is to halt the slide towards irrelevance, had better start listening.

# Notes

## Introduction

1 A second point of note is that, throughout the book, I use the masculine pronoun. This is simply a matter of grammatical preference.

## 1 The Gathering Storm

1 'Residents' fury at former Tory MP's Clacton slur', *Clacton and Frinton Gazette*, 9 September 2014, https://www.clactonandfrintongazette.co.uk/news/11460663.residents-fury-at-former-tory-mps-clacton-slur.

2 BBC *Newsnight*, June 2001; transcript at http://news.bbc.co.uk/1/hi/events/newsnight/1372220.stm.

3 Tony Blair, *A Journey*, Hutchinson, 2010, p. 668.

4 Peter Kellner, 'Labour is not just the party of the working class', YouGov, 16 May 2011, https://yougov.co.uk/topics/politics/articles-reports/2011/05/16/labour-not-just-party-working-class.

5 'How Britain voted in the 2017 election', Ipsos MORI, 20 June 2017, https://www.ipsos.com/ipsos-mori/en-uk/how-britain-voted-2017-election.

6 'How Britain voted at the 2017 general election', YouGov, 13 June 2017, https://yougov.co.uk/topics/poli

tics/articles-reports/2017/06/13/how-britain-voted-2017-general-election.

7   'How Britain voted in the 2019 general election', YouGov, 17 December 2019, https://yougov.co.uk/topics/politics/articles-reports/2019/12/17/how-britain-voted-2019-gen eral-election.

8   Tim Bale, 'Inside Labour's massive membership base', Labour List, 6 October 2017, https://labourlist.org/2017/10/tim-bale-inside-labours-massive-membership-base.

9   'This is an existential moment in Labour's history. It may not survive. And it may never win again', *Guardian*, 20 December 2015, https://www.theguardian.com/comment isfree/2015/dec/20/labour-party-directionless-political-fu ture.

10  Tristram Hunt (ed.), *Labour's Identity Crisis: England and the Politics of Patriotism*, 23 May 2016, p. 61, https://winchester.elsevierpure.com/en/publications/labours-id entity-crisis-england-and-the-politics-of-patriotism-3.

11  Hunt (ed.), *Labour's Identity Crisis*, p. 62.

12  David Goodhart, *The Road to Somewhere: The Populist Revolt and the Future of Politics*, C. Hurst, 2017.

13  'Jon Cruddas: How Labour lost its heart – and heartland', *Independent*, 26 June 2011, https://www.independent.co.uk/news/people/profiles/jon-cruddas-how-labour-lost-its-heart-ndash-and-heartland-2302864.html.

14  John Cruddas, 'A country for old men', *New Statesman*, 7 April 2011, https://www.newstatesman.com/uk-politics/2011/04/english-labour-tradition

15  Department for Business, Energy and Industrial Strategy, *Trade Union Membership 2018: Statistical Bulletin*, https://assets.publishing.service.gov.uk/government/uplo ads/system/uploads/attachment_data/file/805268/trade-un ion-membership-2018-statistical-bulletin.pdf.

16  Office for National Statistics, 'Public sector employment UK, March 2018', https://www.ons.gov.uk/employment andlabourmarket/peopleinwork/publicsectorpersonnel/bulletins/publicsectoremployment/march2018.

17 'Trade union on the 1975 EEC and 2016 EU referendums', BBC News, 19 May 2016, https://www.bbc.co.uk/news/av/uk-politics-36335931/trade-union-on-the-1975-eec-and-2016-eu-referendums.

18 Lord Ashcroft, 'How the United Kingdom voted on Thursday . . . and why', 24 June 2016, http://lordashcroft polls.com/2016/06/how-the-united-kingdom-voted-and-why.

19 Lisa Mckenzie, 'Many working-class people believe in Brexit. Who can blame them?', 31 January 2019, https://blogs.lse.ac.uk/brexit/2019/01/31/many-working-class-people-believe-in-brexit-who-can-blame-them.

20 'How Britain voted in the EU referendum', Ipsos MORI, 5 September 2016, https://www.ipsos.com/ipsos-mori/en-uk/how-britain-voted-2016-eu-referendum.

21 'Did a majority of Conservative and Labour constituencies vote leave in the EU referendum?', Full Fact, 13 July 2018, https://fullfact.org/europe/did-majority-conservative-and-labour-constituencies-vote-leave-eu-referendum.

22 'How MPs voted in the EU referendum', Press Association, 3 November 2016, http://home.bt.com/news/uk-news/how-mps-voted-in-the-eu-referendum-11364110245462.

23 See https://www.youtube.com/watch?v=fOoci0qoW8U.

24 See https://twitter.com/DavidLammy/status/1022243897253289986.

25 'David Lammy says comparing ERG to Nazis "not strong enough"', *Guardian*, 14 April 2019, https://www.theguardian.com/politics/2019/apr/14/comparing-erg-to-nazis-not-strong-enough-says-david-lammy.

26 See https://twitter.com/pollytoynbee/status/1085875822693634048.

27 See https://twitter.com/Andrew_Adonis/status/107825959581606871040.

28 'Brexit: Too many older Leave voters nostalgic for "white" Britain, says Cable', BBC News, 11 March 2018, https://www.bbc.co.uk/news/uk-politics-43364331.

29 'Brexit: Labour MP who said Remain voters were better

educated "has facts on his side"', *Independent*, 30 October 2017, https://www.independent.co.uk/news/uk/politics/brexit-remain-voters-better-educated-labour-mp-barry-sheerman-huddersfield-yougov-facts-leave-a8027121.html.

30  See https://twitter.com/HackedOffHugh/status/1108511401130237952?s=19.

31  'Revoke Article 50 and remain in the EU' petition, https://www.livefrombrexit.com/petitions/241584#bristol-west.

32  See https://twitter.com/RichardDawkins/status/1010775795646779392?s=20

33  Matthew Goodwin, 'The Remainers' caricature of Brexit voters is wrong and shows they still fail to understand why people backed Brexit', Brexit Central, 24 October 2018, https://brexitcentral.com/remainers-caricature-leave-voters-wrong-shows-still-fail-understand-people-backed-brexit.

34  'Minority ethnic attitudes and the 2016 EU referendum', The UK in a Changing Europe, 6 February 2018, https://ukandeu.ac.uk/minority-ethnic-attitudes-and-the-2016-eu-referendum.

35  'EU Referendum result: 7 graphs that explain how Brexit won', *Independent*, 24 June 2016, https://www.independent.co.uk/news/uk/politics/eu-referendum-result-7-graphs-that-explain-how-brexit-won-eu-explained-a7101676.html.

36  Robert Peston, *WTF?*, Hodder & Stoughton, 2017, p. 12.

37  Lord Ashcroft, 'A reminder of how the United Kingdom voted on Thursday – and why', 15 March 2019, http://lordashcroftpolls.com/2019/03/a-reminder-of-how-britain-voted-in-the-eu-referendum-and-why.

38  Matthew Goodwin and Oliver Heath, 'Brexit vote explained: poverty, low skills and lack of opportunities', Joseph Rowntree Foundation, 31 August 2016, https://www.jrf.org.uk/report/brexit-vote-explained-poverty-low-skills-and-lack-opportunities.

39  Centre for Social Justice and Legatum Institute, *48:52 Healing a Divided Britain*, October 2016, p. 2; https://www.centreforsocialjustice.org.uk/library/4852-healing-divided-britain.
40  See https://twitter.com/David_Goodhart/status/1094210 282346418176.
41  Opinium Research poll, 14 August 2018, at https://www.opinium.co.uk/wp-content/uploads/2018/08/VI-14-08-2018-Data-Tables-with-summary-tables.xlsx (see Tab v105).
42  ComRes opinion poll at https://www.comresglobal.com/wp-content/uploads/2019/03/Brexit-Express-Poll-March-2019_updated3.pdf.

## 2 We Need to Talk About Immigration

1  The Migration Observatory at the University of Oxford, 'London: Census Profile', 20 May 2013, https://migrationobservatory.ox.ac.uk/resources/briefings/london-census-profile/
2  'Changing face of Britain: The 77 areas where number of foreign-born people has surged as figures show there are now more Romanians living in the UK than Irish', *Daily Mail*, 24 May 2018, https://www.dailymail.co.uk/news/article-5766219/Population-parts-London-grow-nearly-FIFTH-decade.html.
3  Office for National Statistics, 'Ethnicity and national identity in England and Wales: 2011', https://www.ons.gov.uk/peoplepopulationandcommunity/culturalidentity/ethnicity/articles/ethnicityandnationalidentityinenglandandwales/2012-12-11.
4  Office for National Statistics, 'Ethnic group by Ward, 2001', https://files.datapress.com/london/dataset/ethnic-group-ward-2001/ethnic-group-ward-2001.xls.
5  Office for National Statistics, 'Subnational population predictions for England: 2016-based', https://www.ons.gov.uk/peoplepopulationandcommunity/populationand

migration/populationprojections/bulletins/subnational
populationprojectionsforengland/2016based/pdf.

6 London Datastore (London Assembly), file:///C:/Users/
Paul/Downloads/2016-based%20ethnic%20group%20
projections%20results.pdf%20(1).pdf.

7 London Borough of Barking and Dagenham, 'Population
and Demographic Data', https://www.lbbd.gov.uk/
population-and-demographic-data.

8 London Borough of Barking and Dagenham, 'Population
and Demographic Data', https://www.lbbd.gov.uk/
population-and-demographic-data.

9 See https://www.youtube.com/watch?v=IKf8d4Y-NlM

10 Bank of England, 'The impact of immigration on occupational wages: evidence from Britain', Staff Working Paper
No. 574, December 2015, https://www.bankofengland.
co.uk/-/media/boe/files/working-paper/2015/the-impact-
of-immigration-on-occupational-wages-evidence-from-
britain.pdf?la=en&hash=16F94BC8B55F06967E1F3624
9E90ECE9B597BA9C.

11 Marco Manacorda, Alan Manning and Jonathan
Wadsworth, 'The impact of immigration on the structure
of wages: theory and evidence from Britain', *Journal of
the European Economic Association* 10(1), 2012, https://
onlinelibrary.wiley.com/doi/full/10.1111/j.1542-4774.
2011.01049.x.

12 Chartered Institute of Personnel and Development,
'Labour market outlook: summer 2018', https://www.
cipd.co.uk/Images/lmo-survey-summer2018_tcm18–458
50.pdf.

13 'Hospitality and catering salary offers on the rise as Brexit
looms', The Drinks Business, 6 June 2018, https://www.
thedrinksbusiness.com/2018/06/hospitality-and-catering-
salary-offers-on-the-rise-as-brexit-looms; 'Construction
pay rises as EU workers weigh up leaving UK', *Guardian*,
24 June 2019, https://www.theguardian.com/business/20
19/jun/24/construction-pay-rises-as-eu-workers-weigh-
up-leaving-uk-survey-brexit.

14  Migration Advisory Committee, 'EEA migration in the UK – September 2018', https://assets.publishing.service.gov.uk/government/uploads/system/uploads/attachment_data/file/741926/Final_EEA_report.PDF.

15  'Call for legal protection for wage levels', *Irish Times*, 9 February 2006, https://www.irishtimes.com/news/call-for-legal-protection-for-wage-levels-1.1012783

16  See https://www.youtube.com/watch?v=vf-k6qOfXz0&t=68s.

17  Robert Rowthorn, *The Costs and Benefits of Large-Scale Immigration*, London: Civitas, 2015, p. 21.

18  Rowthorn, *Costs and Benefits*, p. 38.

19  'Romanian hospitals in crisis as emigration takes its toll', *Guardian*, 21 April 2019, https://www.theguardian.com/world/2019/apr/21/romanian-hospitals-in-crisis-as-emigration-take-its-toll.

20  'Latvia: A disappearing nation', Politico, 7 January 2018, https://www.politico.eu/article/latvia-a-disappearing-nation-migration-population-decline.

21  IPPR, *Time for Change: A New Vision for the British Economy*, September 2017, https://www.ippr.org/files/2017–09/1505830437_cej-interim-report-170919.pdf.

22  'Our problem isn't robots, it's the low-wage car-wash economy', *Guardian*, 12 December 2016, https://www.theguardian.com/commentisfree/2016/dec/12/mark-carney-britains-car-wash-economy-low-wage-jobs.

23  'The strawberry-picking robots doing a job humans won't', BBC News, 25 May 2018, https://www.bbc.co.uk/news/business-43816207.

24  Office for National Statistics: https://www.ons.gov.uk/file?uri=/peoplepopulationandcommunity/populationandmigration/internationalmigration/datasets/longterminternationalmigration200citizenshipuk/current/2.00ltimcitizenship1964to2017.xls

25  National Archives, '2011 Census shows non-UK born population of England and Wales continues to rise', 11 December 2012, https://webarchive.nationalarchives.

gov.uk/20160107123603/http://www.ons.gov.uk/ons/
rel/census/2011-census/key-statistics-for-local-authorit
ies-in-england-and-wales/sty-non-uk-born-population.
html.

26 'British want EU migrants to stay after Brexit, says poll',
*Guardian*, 21 August 2016, https://www.theguardian.
com/world/2016/aug/21/migration-poll-eu-workers-brex
it.

27 M. D. R. Evans and Jonathan Kelly, 'Prejudice against
immigrants symptomizes a larger syndrome', *Frontiers in
Sociology*, 26 February 2019, at https://www.frontiersin.
org/articles/10.3389/fsoc.2019.00012/full.

28 'Attitudes towards immigration after Windrush', Ipsos
MORI, 26 May 2018, https://www.ipsos.com/ipsos-mori/
en-uk/attitudes-towards-immigration-after-windrush.

29 Centre for Social Justice and Legatum Institute, *48:52
Healing a Divided Britain*, October 2016, p. 12, https://
www.centreforsocialjustice.org.uk/library/4852-heal
ing-divided-britain.

30 NatCen Social Research, 'British social attitudes 2013:
Attitudes to immigration', http://www.natcen.ac.uk/
media/205569/immigration-bsa31.pdf.

31 See https://www.jfklibrary.org/learn/about-jfk/the-kenn
edy-family/robert-f-kennedy/robert-f-kennedy-speeches/
remarks-at-the-university-of-kansas-march-18-1968.

32 'Don't listen to the whingers – London needs immigrants', *Evening Standard*, 23 October 2009, https://
www.standard.co.uk/news/dont-listen-to-the-whingers-
london-needs-immigrants-6786170.html.

### 3 A New National Religion: Liberal Wokedom

1 See https://twitter.com/BBCNewsbeat/status/953602152
311803905.

2 'The truth about young people and Brexit', BBC Three,
5 October 2018, https://www.bbc.co.uk/bbcthree/article/
b8d097b0–3ad4–4dd9-aa25-af6374292de0.

3 Eric Kaufmann, 'The Great Awokening started a century ago', UnHerd, 13 January 2020, https://unherd.com/2020/01/the-great-awokening-started-a-century-ago.

4 'Trans inmate jailed for Wakefield prison sex offences', BBC News, 11 October 2018, https://www.bbc.co.uk/news/uk-england-leeds-45825838.

5 See https://twitter.com/mayor_anderson/status/1030878562147094530.

6 'Police response to transphobic stickers branded extraordinary', *Daily Telegraph*, 14 October 2019, https://www.telegraph.co.uk/news/2019/10/14/police-response-transphobic-stickers-branded-extraordinary.

7 'Maya Forstater: Woman loses tribunal over transgender tweets', BBC News, 19 December 2019, https://www.bbc.co.uk/news/uk-50858919.

8 See *Forstater v CGD* judgment at https://assets.publishing.service.gov.uk/media/5e15e7f8e5274a06b555b8b0/Maya_Forstater__vs_CGD_Europe__Centre_for_Global_Development_and_Masood_Ahmed_-_Judgment.pdf.

9 'Lincolnshire man challenges police transphobia guidelines', BBC News, 6 August 2019, https://www.bbc.co.uk/news/uk-england-lincolnshire-49249142.

10 'Danny Baker fired from BBC Radio 5 Live over "racist" royal baby tweet', *Daily Mirror*, 9 May 2019, https://www.mirror.co.uk/3am/celebrity-news/breaking-danny-baker-fired-bbc-15019097.

11 See https://stopfundinghate.info/about-the-campaign.

12 Home Office, *Hate Crime, England and Wales, 2018/19*, https://assets.publishing.service.gov.uk/government/uploads/system/uploads/attachment_data/file/839172/hate-crime-1819-hosb2419.pdf.

13 West Yorkshire Police website: https://www.westyorkshire.police.uk/advice/abuse-anti-social-behaviour/hate-crime/hate-crime-hate-incidents; Citizens Advice website: https://www.citizensadvice.org.uk/law-and-courts/discrimination/hate-crime/what-are-hate-incidents-and-hate-crime.

14 See https://twitter.com/DawnButlerBrent/status/118929 2693593169920?s=20.

15 See https://twitter.com/brexitcentral/status/1176137195 352207366.

16 'Britain was complacent about the far right. Now it's out in force', *Guardian*, 5 October 2019, https://www. theguardian.com/commentisfree/2019/oct/05/britain-far-right-oswald-mosley-bbc-platform.

17 See https://twitter.com/ElspethElspeth/status/97683042 7007737861.

18 'Joking about vowels is a hate crime now', *The Spectator*, 21 April 2018, https://www.spectator.co.uk/2018/04/a-joke-about-welsh-vowels-is-a-hate-crime-say-the-tupp enny-panjandrums.

19 'Sadiq Khan launches London online hate crime hub', BBC News, 24 April 2017, https://www.bbc.co.uk/news/uk-england-london-39692811.

20 'Police arresting nine people a day in fight against web trolls', *The Times*, 12 October 2017, https://www.the times.co.uk/article/police-arresting-nine-people-a-day-in-fight-against-web-trolls-b8nkpgp2d.

21 'Anna Soubry: Speaker urges police to tackle MP harassment', BBC News, 8 January 2019, https://www.bbc. co.uk/news/uk-politics-46789601.

22 'Protester who harassed Anna Soubry handed suspended sentence', *Guardian*, 22 July 2019, https://www.the guardian.com/uk-news/2019/jul/22/protester-who-hara ssed-anna-soubry-handed-suspended-sentence.

23 'David Lammy says comparing ERG to Nazis "not strong enough"', *Guardian*, 14 April 2019, https://www.the guardian.com/politics/2019/apr/14/comparing-erg-to-nazis-not-strong-enough-says-david-lammy.

24 'Brexit supporter is jailed for 28 days for harassing Remainer ex-MP Anna Soubry', *Daily Mail*, 16 December 2019, https://www.dailymail.co.uk/news/art icle-7798375/Pro-Brexit-Amy-Dalla-Mura-jailed-28-da ys-harassing-ex-MP-Anna-Soubry-BBC-interview.html.

25 'Pensioner fears police raid after Tory MP Antoinette Sandbach reported her to cops for grumbling email', *The Sun*, 9 June 2018, https://www.thesun.co.uk/news/ 6487476/antoinette-sanbach-tory-mp-eddisbury-cheshi re-police-email.

26 'Police called after Stella Creasy targeted by anti-abortion group', *Guardian*, 28 September 2019, https://www. theguardian.com/world/2019/sep/28/labour-mp-stella-creasy-targeted-by-anti-abortion-group.

27 'Police "should be neutral" in sex abuse inquiries, says Met head', BBC News, 11 February 2016, https://www. bbc.co.uk/news/uk-35546690.

## 4 The Case for the Nation State

1 Branko Milanović, *Global Inequality: A New Approach for the Age of Globalization*, Harvard University Press, 2018.

2 Credit Suisse, *Global Wealth Report 2019*, https://www. credit-suisse.com/about-us/en/reports-research/global-we alth-report.html.

3 Paul Krugman, 'Capital control freaks', Slate, 27 September 1999, https://slate.com/business/1999/09/capi tal-control-freaks.html.

4 'IMF drops opposition to capital controls', *Financial Times*, 3 December 2012, https://www.ft.com/content/e6 20482e-3d5c-11e2-9e13-00144feabdc0.

5 The full essay can be found at https://www.orwell.ru/ library/essays/lion/english/e_eye.

6 Jan Eichhorn, 'Identification with Englishness is the best clue to understanding support for Brexit', https://blogs. lse.ac.uk/politicsandpolicy/the-black-box-of-brexit-ident ification-with-englishness-is-the-best-clue.

7 'England and the structurally screwed', *Huffington Post*, 31 October 2017, https://www.huffingtonpost.co.uk/ anthony-barnett/england-structurally-screwed-brexit_b_ 18426384.html.

8   See https://twitter.com/centrefortowns/status/100901783
    2397471745/photo/1.
9   'The English question: Young are less proud to be
    English', BBC News, 3 June 2018, at https://www.bbc.
    co.uk/news/uk-england-44142843.
10  English Labour Network, *General Election 2019: How
    Labour Lost England*, February 2020, at https://englishla
    bournetwork.files.wordpress.com/2020/03/ge2019-how-
    labour-lost-england-pdf.pdf.

## 5  What is to Be Done?

1   Tim Bale, 'Inside Labour's massive membership base',
    Labour List, 6 October 2017, at https://labourlist.org/
    2017/10/tim-bale-inside-labours-massive-membership-
    base.
2   John Mills, *Raising Productivity*, February 2018, at
    https://d3n8a8pro7vhmx.cloudfront.net/labourleave/pag
    es/1749/attachments/original/1521320580/RaisingProdu
    ctivity_WEB.pdf?1521320580.
3   John Mills, *A Competitive Pound for a Stronger Economy*,
    London: Civitas, 2013, at https://civitas.org.uk/content/
    files/JohnMillsCompetitivePound.pdf.
4   Centre for Social Justice, *Fractured Families*, at https://
    www.centreforsocialjustice.org.uk/library/fractured-fami
    lies-stability-matters.
5   Centre for Social Justice, *Family Breakdown*, at https://
    www.centreforsocialjustice.org.uk/policy/breakthrough-
    britain/family-breakdown.

# Index

214

# Index

Left and wider
establishment's attempts to
thwart, 46
Left's opposition to, 43–4,
151
liberal intelligentsia's aversion
to, 47–8
public criticism of MPs,
126–9
as a reaction to globalisation,
155
reflection of public opposition
to open borders, 191
Revoke Article 50 petition,
48
roots in cultural revolution,
18
scaremongering by Remain
campaign, 41
seen by liberals and
progressives as victory for
'nativism', 140
significance of economic
factors in referendum, 52
support among BAME voters,
49–50
vote driven by anger of
neglected communities,
16–17, 39–42
Brexit Party, 121
British National Party, 26, 66,
71, 91, 120
British Social Attitudes Survey
2013, 87
British Union of Fascists, 121
Brown, Gordon, 32
Butler, Dawn, 121

Cable, Vince, 48
Cameron, David, 70
Castle, Barbara, 43
Centre for Social Justice, 51, 87,
188–90
Centre for Towns, 167
Change UK, 36

Chartered Institute of Personnel
and Development, 74
Chartists, 127, 163
Christian socialism, 21–2
Churchill, Winston, 181
Clacton-on-Sea, 17, 67–8
Clarke, Charles, 21
Conservative Party, 25–7,
35, 40, 54, 167–8, 170,
177–80
Cook, James (Captain), 56
Co-operative movement, 22,
183
Corbyn, Jeremy, 26, 36–7, 171,
178, 184
Covid-19 pandemic, 142–3,
159, 180
Cox, Jo, 127
Creasy, Stella, 129–30
credit unions, 183
Cricket World Cup, 2019, 85
Crow, Bob, 43
Cruddas, Jon, 34
cultural revolution, 18–20, 113

Dagenham Girl Pipers, 57
Dalla Mura, Amy, 129
Dawkins, Richard, 48
Delors, Jacques, 43
Denham, John, 168
devolution, 160, 166–7
Diggers, 169
Dimbleby, David, 70
Duffy, Gillian, 32
Dumbleton, Pam, 69–70

employee share ownership
schemes, 184–5
English Labour Network, 168,
175
European Research Group, 128
European Union
anti-socialist institution, 43
attempts to replicate national
solidarity, 158–9

215

# Index

# Index

# Index